Something to Live for

Something to Live for

my
postnatal
depression and
how the NHS
saved
us

LAURA CANTY

monoray

First published in Great Britain in 2021 by Monoray,
an imprint of Octopus Publishing Group Ltd,
Carmelite House, 50 Victoria Embankment,
London EC4Y 0DZ
www.octopusbooks.co.uk
www.octopusbooksusa.com

An Hachette UK Company
www.hachette.co.uk

Distributed in the US by Hachette Book Group,
1290 Avenue of the Americas, 4th and 5th Floors, New York, NY 10104

Distributed in Canada by Canadian Manda Group,
664 Annette St, Toronto, Ontario, Canada M6S 2C8

ISBN 978-1-91318-365-3

A CIP catalogue record for this book is available from the British Library.

Printed and bound in the UK.

1 3 5 7 9 10 8 6 4 2

This FSC® label means that materials used for
the product have been responsibly sourced.

To Rhys, Becca and Ellie.
You lived my pain.
You cast no judgement.
You were tirelessly there,
every step of the way.

CONTENTS

INTRODUCTION

This is a book about hope.

It's the story of my family's struggle with mental illness after the birth of our son, but above all it's about how the love of good friends and family, and our incredible NHS, brought me back from the brink of a life-threatening illness.

My story is similar to that of millions. I'm not a celebrity; I am an ordinary new mum living an ordinary life. My husband and I both work five days a week, we discuss what we're going to have for dinner most days and we eat out or have a takeaway probably once or twice a week. I sensibly married a builder so we live in our renovated, mid-30s, semi-detached house in a quiet street, and our bin day is Thursday.

My pregnancy was on the whole totally fine. I had morning sickness for about 12 weeks, a brief respite and then suffered with indigestion and heartburn until our son was born. At my 38-week check-up, I was diagnosed with pre-eclampsia and taken straight to the hospital. About 12 hours later, after induction and an emergency caesarean section, our baby boy was born. We always knew he was going to be called Arthur after his great-grandfather.

When Arthur was about four weeks old, my mental health started to go downhill rapidly. I stopped being able to function and I was basically scared of everything, not least our son. In this book I want to show you how I went from a fairly confident new mum to someone who couldn't sleep, wouldn't go out and couldn't bear to look at her baby. As painful as it is, I want to take you inside my head and help you understand what it feels like to have totally fallen apart, malfunctioned, broken down.

I was diagnosed by our GP with postnatal depression and anxiety. The local Perinatal Mental Health Team tried to treat me at home for eight weeks until, one day, I decided to kill myself. It was at this point that I was referred for one of the precious beds at a Mother and Baby Unit (MBU).

Not many people know about MBUs because they're not something we tend to talk about. They are psychiatric units specially set up to treat mothers with postnatal-related mental health illness while keeping their babies with them. I was lucky enough to be allocated a bed shortly after referral and it was here that I was fortunate enough to receive accelerated, specialist care for my illness. But many do not. In fact, many don't receive any treatment at all. This might be because they are never diagnosed – either through shame, fear or just because postnatal illness was missed by their healthcare professional – or because there isn't a bed available for them at a time when they need it, close enough to where they live.

The thing about MBUs is that they give you 24/7 care. They allow you to recover the sleep debt that contributes to so many cases of postnatal illness, while the staff support you in caring for your baby. They ensure you get the correct medication, changing your drugs quickly while monitoring you until the right mix is found. They also offer talking therapies with a psychologist to give you coping strategies and a routine of self-care for when you're discharged. In my case, I even received physiotherapy to help with an old knee injury to ensure I could keep up running.

The care and attention I got saved my life. But here's the thing: there are only around 151 beds spread across 19 of these units in England, and the average stay is approximately 8 weeks. That's why I consider myself lucky. (Incidentally, there are only 2 units in Scotland and none at all in Wales and Ireland.)

In this book I'm going to take you into the hospital and give you a glimpse of the staff who work tirelessly, night and day, to mend broken people. I'm going to show you the other patients, whose stories were just as extraordinary – and ordinary – as my own. I'm going to take you through the day-to-day life of the unit, the treatments, the visitors and how I started believing in myself enough to be allowed 'home leave' and eventually be discharged.

Yes, there is no doubt this hospital saved my life, no doubt at all. It was and continues to be an amazing facility staffed by the most special people – somewhere that will always bring a tear to my eye when I think of what it did for Arthur and me. I hope that by the time you have finished reading this book, it will hold a special place for you, too.

As I was so grateful for the help I received, I now volunteer with the NHS, supporting women going through the same devastating but frighteningly common experience as me. The message I get time after time is that postnatal depression (PND) is one of the few areas of mental health we are still not talking about. Take a look around. Mothers all around you are suffering from PND without you realising it. Some of them are ill enough to be admitted to hospital. But many of them are getting up every day, putting their makeup on and pretending everything is okay. They are keeping quiet because, while it's increasingly acceptable to say you're not okay, it's still not acceptable to say you want to kill yourself or you want to give your baby away.

The worst shame I felt about PND wasn't admitting I was one of the one-in-five women who suffer from it, that I wanted to end my life, or even that I wanted harm to come to my baby. The worst shame was from the ripple effect I had on my world. The stress and torment I caused my husband, my family and my friends – that I will never be able to take away or find any suitable way of apologising for. Coupled with this is the knowledge that I cost the NHS thousands and thousands of pounds in diagnosing me, treating me, and housing and feeding me for nearly three months in one of their most specialist facilities.

It took a small army of people – professional and personal – to put me back together and I have made it my mission to spend the rest of my life giving back. Sharing my story with whoever wants to hear it is a step towards 'normalising' PND and making it more acceptable for other women to admit to having it. It is my hope that this will help others to receive the treatment they need rather than suffering in silence. In turn, I guess this makes it worth all the suffering I have caused. I figure that something good has to come of me dragging the people in my little world through the most painful six months of their lives.

All I kept asking for when I was in the depths of the illness was hope. Hope that I would get better, hope that we would be a family again, hope that this wouldn't always be the way things were. If I couldn't have hope, then there really was no point in being alive. I can't count the number of nurses, doctors, friends, family members and even strangers who told me the same thing: 'You will get better'. But all I could think was, *How do you know?* I knew they had seen other people get better, but what if I was the one who didn't? I would beg anyone who would listen: 'Show me a me-shaped person who has got through this and I will believe there is hope.' They simply couldn't.

My hope now, therefore, is that by writing this book I will expose my story to the largest number of people I can and that maybe I can be at least one other sufferer's 'me-shaped person', offering them the hope that they will get better.

I'm fed up of seeing photographs of young families apparently having the time of their lives. Maybe they are in that moment, but I can guarantee it's only half the picture. These photos were part of my downfall, showing me how things 'should be' once you have a baby and not in any way related to my truth. I would obsess over them and constantly ask myself, 'Why me?'

I want to show that PND doesn't discriminate over who it affects, it's more common than you think and there is absolutely no shame in admitting that it got you. By baring my soul, I want to explain what motherhood is like for some women. I hate the thought of anyone else going through this. I know that hearing my story will not necessarily make their suffering less, but it might make them feel less alone.

It was the psychologist in hospital who suggested that I start to write some of my story down. I was constantly asking 'Why me?' so she suggested it as a way of processing what was happening.

Putting this book together from those notes and all the information I could glean from WhatsApp messages, calendar entries, photographs and conversations with my friends and family has allowed me to come up with a timeline of events from Arthur's birth to me being discharged from hospital. As I've relived those moments – the suicidal thoughts, the fear and the exhaustion – I've cried, smirked and felt the goosebumps all over again. It's helped me not only to realise how poorly I was but how much I really do care about this stuff. Postnatal depression is the worst, most evil illness I have ever had the misfortune to come across, and although I know it's not realistic to think that it won't happen to other mothers, if there is any way I can make it less horrible, less exhausting, less stressful, less lonely and less hopeless, I will.

Oh, and I should say that many of the names have been changed and a couple of people have been combined into characters. I would have loved to namecheck the amazing staff and patients on The Chamomile Suite, but for obvious reasons I need to respect people's personal and professional privacy. And 'amazing' doesn't even cut it. They helped me to heal, to learn to love my baby and to understand that, no matter how broken you are, there is always something to live for. I hope you are all well and realise that not only were you part of my journey, but I will never forget you for the kindness and compassion you showed me.

All of my close friends and family have been depicted as who they are and, in a tiny way, this is a massive thank you to you for being part of my army. You were there, you were with us and you were part of getting me back to being the wife, daughter, sister and friend that you all know. I love each and every one of you, very much.

LAURA CANTY

A NIGHTLY DEATH

My absolute favourite part of my day was the few minutes between taking the tablet and falling into a deep sleep. I always thought it was a shame that you couldn't feel how good the sleep was or how long it actually lasted as it always ended the same way – with me springing awake when Rhys walked into the room bringing Arthur to bed. Then I'd feel the same sense of dread that I'd felt just a few seconds before taking the tablet, the dread that was pretty much my constant state. Rhys would do the right thing, try to shhhh me to sleep like he had done with Arthur, but my body wouldn't let me rest as my mind was constantly questioning: what if this, or that, or what if I don't do this but do that, will this lead to a different outcome? Analyse, analyse, analyse…I'd question him as if he could give me definitive black-and-white answers. How long has Arthur been asleep? When did he last feed? How much did he have? How much did he spew up? I was ultimately asking

Rhys what kind of a night I was in for. The reality didn't really matter. Now I had been bumped out of my drug-induced sleep, there was very little chance of me getting back there. I'd start trying to work out the half-life of the sleeping drug in the hope that there would still be some sleep-inducing chemical left in my body. I wasn't allowed a larger dose as I would be doing all the night feeds, scared my sleep-deprived builder husband would fall off a scaffold if he were to do any. Plus, I was now awake, and he had been injected with that new-dad hormone that meant he could sleep through anything. My dad had warned me about that.

I would never quite know when to get up for Arthur in the night and this really, really frustrated me. Was that a cry or just a murmur? Does he really need food or is he just having a snuffle? How long has it been since his last feed? People say to only get up to a cry – why can't I work out if this is a cry? It's my own flipping baby, how can I not have identified what kind of cry that is? The common sinking feeling would flood my body and I'd justify any and every reason not to get out of bed. Or, if it was still dark, I'd just think, *Get up and feed him, then you'll be allowed to get straight back into bed, put ear plugs in and try to fall into that dreamless sleep where you can forget all of the things that are making you worry.* I loved the darkness, darkness meant I was allowed to be in bed. Light meant I'd feel like I should be up and about, living the new-family dream that had been sold to me a million times over, on TV, on social media, in life.

When the sun came up and the room started to fill with light, I'd want to actually push it back around to Australia. Give them more of a day, we don't really want one over here, thanks. I'd hear the milkman's float buzz past, which meant it was 04:30. The next milestone to the world creeping awake was the neighbour's motorbike kicking into life, shortly followed by Rhys getting up for work and then the front door banging as he went to take our dog for a walk. Sometimes, if the timing was right, he'd also pop Arthur in the sling and take him to the park, but only if it coincided with a feed just finishing and we could guarantee (who am I kidding, nothing is guaranteed with kids) that he wouldn't need a feed any time soon. This was the only real time my mind and body would allow me to drift off naturally. I must have given myself permission, knowing that the baby was actually out of the house and I wasn't needed. Rhys took everything in his stride, took things on, adapted, learned how to do new things, kept going, but I was completely shut off to all of it.

When the sun was eventually up, I'd torture myself by repeatedly telling myself to get up. I'd writhe around, watch the pigeons on the aerial, think about what it would be like to be a pigeon, writhe the other way, pull the covers over my head and curl up as small as I could, then fling the covers off and jump out only to jump straight back in again. A ridiculously drawn-out routine, slightly different each day, but still performed every single morning, without fail. When eventually I did get up and tiptoe to Arthur's cot at the end of the room, if I saw his eyes were closed, I'd crawl straight back into my bed. I'm sure the speed I could achieve from the cot back to the bed was some kind of record, I was so very keen to be back in, safe under the covers. There was something very safe indeed about being in my bed. I just wanted to be there all of the time.

All of it.

CHAPTER 1

COMING HOME

3RD JUNE

After four nights in hospital following my emergency caesarean section, my blood pressure has stabilised and I'm discharged. I leave with a bag of goodies – painkillers, blood-pressure tablets and iron tablets – and the obligatory photo of Rhys carrying the car seat out of the hospital. I post it on social media, professing how ecstatically in love with life I am. And I am. Or at least, I should be. To be honest, I don't really feel much at all. I'm just going through the motions, doing the things I think I should be doing.

When we get inside, I think how much life has changed. Everything looks the same, but it's like I've entered another world from the one where I merrily skipped off to my 38-week appointment thinking I had another two weeks of chilling until the baby's expected due date. As soon as the midwife tested my wee at that appointment, her face

13

changed and she said, 'I think you'll be having your baby today'. Rhys came to get me from work, still covered in building bits, and drove me home as I insisted on grabbing some flip-flops for the hospital bag. I waddled into the house and up to the bedroom to have a few seconds to myself, looking around and at the empty Next-to-Me crib thinking, *There will be a baby in here next time I'm in this room.*

Rhys shouted, snapping me out of it, so I grabbed my flip-flops and off we went.

I felt a sense of excitement then. I was excited for our new chapter, something we both wanted and the next natural thing to do when you've been together and 'run out of things to chat about' (Billy Connolly). I knew we'd have a long engagement, so baby it was. But now he's here I don't feel excited, I feel anxious, scared and daunted by what is to come.

Pregnancy was a bit like this. I'd have waves of thinking what it would be like to have a baby and what the sleep deprivation would be like, but I pushed those thoughts out of my head thinking I'll deal with that when it happens. Apart from the sickness, the excruciating heartburn that hit me at about 20 weeks and the swollen ankles (that turned out to be pre-eclampsia), I generally thought being pregnant was okay. I felt special and people smiled at me in the street.

We pop the car seat on the floor and let Alma have a little sniff of the baby. She's not interested. A spaniel, she's only interested in tennis balls and humans she can wrestle.

She's just pleased to have us home and, conscious of her feeling jealous, I make a big fuss of her. She gives me a good sniff: the new hospital-smelling mummy. I sit on the sofa and message the antenatal group, telling them we're home. We're the fourth of eight to have had our baby and saw the fifth as we were leaving the hospital!

Later, my dad visits briefly. I can't believe he's driven all the way from Yorkshire (where I grew up and my northern roots herald from) to see us for a couple of hours, but I'm pleased he has, it's a chance to talk about something other than baby. Rhys is changing Arthur's nappy when Dad arrives and when he brings him into the living room, Dad bursts into tears. I'm pretty shocked, this isn't the sort of thing my dad would do.

But I don't feel anything inside, myself. Not for the baby, or for my crying dad. *That's odd*, I remember thinking. I thought I was the one who was supposed to be awash with hormones! I guess it means so much to him and that's nice. And he says he can't believe how well we all look. That's the adrenaline, I tell him.

Rhys cooks dinner of salmon, new potatoes and vegetables and I light a candle. We have a romantic first dinner at home while our five-day-old baby sleeps in his Moses basket on the kitchen table. This is easy, I think. We've got this.

The first night at home with a baby is odd. Over your entire life, you've been used to going to bed at going-to-bed time and sleeping until your alarm wakes you and you remember it's time for work. Then at the weekend, you try to lie in, but you end up waking at the same time as your weekday alarm and tossing and turning until you're so frustrated that you get up. Of course, you experience nights of poor sleep at times, maybe because you're worried about something, you're in a new place, have jet lag or an illness. But these things don't last for ever, so you just have a good night's sleep the next night and everything is fixed.

But when you come home with a baby, you find yourself staring down the barrel of never having a full eight hours of sleep again, ever, in your whole life. Or at least that's how it felt to me.

A baby born by caesarean section sleeps differently from a baby born through the regular route. As the baby's not been squeezed and squashed the way nature intended, its lungs are still so full of gunk that it's like trying to sleep next to a snuffling piglet. As soon as you stop hearing the snuffles, you wake, worrying that the baby has somehow slipped into a coma.

The first time Arthur wakes for milk, I feel like I've been asleep for four minutes. It's like my eyes are welded shut. I try to sit up, but the excruciating pain from my cut-up abdomen screams at me. I realise for the very first time that it's no longer about me. I need drugs, sleep, healing vibes and I probably should try to squeeze out a wee, but instead I have to get up and feed this baby as the screams won't get less and no one else is going to do it. It's incredibly hard to sit up in bed without using your stomach muscles. But I'm starting to adapt, working out ways I can get into a position to be able to feed.

Then I decide to change his nappy because maybe that's why he's screaming, and I think that while I'm awake I'll wind him, go for a wee and check my social media to see how many more likes I have from previously announcing I'm home from hospital. Finally, I settle him again in his crib and try to get some more sleep.

An hour later, it all happens again. But I'm getting into the swing of it. I'm coping.

4TH JUNE

Rhys's mum and stepdad, Alison and Bernard, are over from Australia, and come back from their first tour of England to meet Arthur. Their tour included a trip to see my mum, Julia, and stepdad, George, in Hull (the motherland) and I enjoy hearing how they are doing, and that Hull is the same as when I left it. Alison and Bernard came over when I was right at the end of pregnancy and helped us finish off bits for the house, culminating in the obligatory Ikea run for the final things we needed (lamps, changing mat, tealights). I'm not sure what I was thinking either, but nesting is a powerful, all-encompassing, real feeling.

They come round for a barbecue this evening and insist that I don't lift a finger. Apparently, I have the most important job of anyone here, so I just need to concentrate on that! That's not what I think. Sitting down and feeding a baby is much easier than cooking for and cleaning up after four adults.

5TH JUNE

When the sun comes up and your partner is still on paternity leave, it's easy to get enthusiastic about having a new baby. Who needs sleep while you have so much adrenaline in your body and loads of lovely people are popping round with cards, gifts and baked goods? We go out to the park, we fill out the baby book, we eat sugar constantly and life is good.

7TH JUNE

We have an appointment with the doctor today. As I had pre-eclampsia, they are continuing to monitor my blood pressure. It took a while to get it under control in hospital after a couple of faints, so I'm pleased they are keeping an eye on me now I'm out. First real test, I take a deep breath and wheel Arthur in his pram down the ramp Rhys has made for us outside the front door. I try not to look at the mud pit which is the remains of our front garden after months and months of skips residing there. Arthur has just fed and is asleep, so I'm mega-chuffed at the timing. As we sit in the steamy waiting room, proud to be early for our appointment, a number of people smile at me. It turns out people, generally older ladies, love mums as much as they love pregnant ladies. I wonder if this would have happened in a waiting room if we still lived in London and count my lucky stars we are in Cheltenham.

When I was done with London, my company had an office 'out west' so I asked for a transfer thinking it would be a nicer (cheaper) place to bring up a family. Cheltenham soon became home. It's a lovely and pretty normal town with a Starbucks and a Maccers and it's a relief people actually acknowledge each other, smile if you run past them, hold a door open, you know.

Anyway, we sit in silence, both trying to gather our thoughts, or that's what I assume – I have no idea what's going on in Rhys' head most of the time. Ten minutes after the appointment was scheduled, Arthur starts to stir, which turns into full-scale crying. I look at Rhys, half in panic and half for an answer. People are looking. I know I have to breastfeed him, and I know without looking up that I'm sat opposite a chap. A sinking feeling floods over me – am I just going to man up and do this? I can't, my boob will be about two metres from his face. I turn the chair around and as I lift Arthur out of the pram there is an audible gasp from a couple of people in the waiting room, followed by a chorus of 'awww'. I can hear them discussing how he must be newly born and I want to catch their eye and tell them he is. I have a little fight with a giant muslin but eventually win and get Arthur latched, which is a massive relief.

At that moment, the doctor opens the door and calls our name. I casually try to bundle everything up and stroll into the doctor's office. Rhys is bringing up the rear with all the other paraphernalia we have brought with us 'just in case' and I'm proud of us. Feeding and walking, tick, I've got this.

The doctor apologises for running late and we tell her not to worry, we have all the time in the world right now.

The instant I sit down, I'm not listening to the doctor as I'm worried I have made the bloke in the waiting room feel uncomfortable for turning the chair away from him. *Stop overthinking things, Laura, I'm sure he was too involved in his phone to notice.* And anyway, I know I have a habit of overthinking and overanalysing. This is one of those times. *It really doesn't matter. You have a little baby and you are coping. It's just fine.*

The appointment is quick, my blood pressure is slightly high, so I have to stay on the tablets. Gutted. The midwife has told me they could be affecting my sleep and general fogginess so I'm really looking forward to getting off them. There is so much more physically to having a baby than just your tummy growing and the exit hole needing a bit of TLC. This has just dawned on me and I wish I had known before. Not that it would have changed my mind about having a baby, I just like all the facts, thank you.

8TH JUNE

Mum's come to visit and she's like a whirlwind. I can hardly keep my eyes on her. I know she's trying to help, and I did desperately want my pasta cupboard rearranging but I'm finding it all a bit exhausting. I know she's full of adrenaline too, but I wish she could take a moment to take it in, take her first grandchild in; she's not visiting for long.

That afternoon also sees our Tupperware drawer and under-the-sink cupboard get some much-needed attention and, yes, it feels nice to be all rearranged and clean and tidy but I wish Mum would drink Arthur in while she's here.

10TH JUNE

When I walk into the kitchen, I'm greeted with the smell of baking. I understand from Rhys that Mum was up until about midnight making us chocolate cake, vanilla sponge and some scones just for good measure. I open the freezer and see we probably have enough scones to feed visitors until Arthur is about two. I also notice most of the kitchen cupboards now have some order to them and are lined with kitchen roll. She should have shares in kitchen roll. I guess she's been taken right back to when she was a first-time mum and she just wants to help, doing whatever.

I had grand plans for batch-cooking meals for us to stock the freezer with, but never got around to that before Arthur made an early appearance.

I love Mum and I wish she lived around the corner. I know she has to go back home today to be with George and I totally get it – his next chemo appointment is tomorrow – but every single ounce of me wishes she lived down the road. I should be supporting her, but I just want to lean on her.

We exchange texts and photos during her whole journey home – I guess it kind of makes me feel like she's still here. It makes me less sad that she's gone and that I don't know when she'll be able to come back. I can't believe she's not fallen asleep on the train; she must be exhausted.

12TH JUNE

There's a knock at the door and I remember that the health visitor who called to introduce herself last week is due to come today. Alma gives her a good sniff. She comes in and doesn't seem too bothered that the dog now has her nose in her handbag, so I think she's probably a good sort. She weighs Arthur and tells me what her role is. She then fusses over Alma and, as we say goodbye, she tells me she'll be coming next week. I'm not sure why as the midwives are still coming every day to check my blood pressure. But who am I to question how things work, I've never been here before.

Later that day, the midwife does indeed pop round to take my blood pressure. I love having them drop in. It's so comforting to know that someone who knows about baby stuff is coming every day, but I just don't know how they are managing it along with their baby-delivering duties. I did offer to go into the hospital to have my blood pressure checked, but they know I have had a caesarean section and they are midwives, so they are among the kindest people on the planet. They support families through life-changing times and know just what to say when women are experiencing the most heightened emotions they will ever feel. No one likes a hormonal woman, but midwives are not only able to work with them, they have a way of making them feel so reassured. They are a special sort.

13TH JUNE

Today is the day we go to the registry office to register Arthur's birth. This is the first trip out since returning from hospital that has involved the car. When we've wandered out to the park, I haven't cared what I look like as it's just a park in the middle of the day and I have a pram with me, a visible excuse to anyone who thinks I look like I've not slept and can't remember how to dress myself. But registering the birth is a thing, a milestone, one we need to remember and one where we might see actual real non-park people, so I put on a maternity dress and feel okay, quite nice actually. My hair is in a mum-bun but that's okay as it's hot outside. Rhys is as chilled as ever – in fact, I'm sure there is a graph with crossing lines that shows the more chilled he is, the more stressed and wound up I am.

Anyway, we get in the car and drive there. I feel like I'm in a whole new Cheltenham, a Cheltenham that exists with me as a mum, one I have never experienced before. I have obviously completely forgotten how to get to the registry office, so we take a wrong turn at first but eventually arrive and park up two minutes before our appointment time. We need to feed the meter but, obviously, neither of us has coins and the meter seems to be about a mile away. I say I'll go in with Arthur on my own but then freak out as that means I'll be with Arthur on my own. Rhys downloads the parking app while I just stand on the street, sweating.

When we eventually make it to the office, the lady on reception is understanding and says that with babies, they never expect the appointments to run on time. Phew, we are not the worst parents ever and why on earth did they not say that in the letter?

Arthur is registered, a proper person. I want to celebrate our achievement, so we go to the Hotel du Vin nearby where I lose my breast-feeding-in-public virginity (the doctor's waiting room doesn't count) and inhale a steak sandwich and chips. I'm not sure when I last ate a proper, savoury lunch. I waddle to the loo to make sure I've put everything away where it should be and that nothing is leaking. I change my enormous maternity pad and stare at myself in the mirror. The last time I was in this hotel, staring into this mirror, I was applying red lipstick ready to go back out into the work Christmas do. That now seems like a million years ago.

Shortly after we get home, my friends Bec and Ellie arrive with bags of food. It's the first time I've seen them at home and it's nice to do something normal. Kate, Bec's partner, is desperate to come and meet Arthur apparently but since they had their son, Jude, we only get one of them for an evening while the other stays in while Jude sleeps. Kate's going to pop around tomorrow if that's okay? Of course it is, let's flood the house with normal things, things we used to do pre-Arthur, I'm all up for that.

They are here to cook us dinner and I love them for this. They do everything, including feeding me (à la The Rock) while I breastfeed Arthur. I feel like I have a glimpse back into my old life. The house is full of laughter, good food and drink and I feel content. I tell myself that when I'm having a bad day, I need to think of this meal, of Rhys and of my best friends and life will be okay again.

14TH JUNE

My big brother Tom is supposed to be coming for dinner tonight to meet his nephew, but I just don't think I can face it. I have been up for what feels like all night and I can't stop crying today. I think the adrenaline has well and truly been used up. I know he's my brother and he won't care but I guess I still have some semblance of pride as I pick up my phone to text him. He doesn't need to see his sister in this much of a mess, especially as he's not had children and if he was thinking of it, I'm sure I would single-handedly put him off!

People had warned me about 'the day you won't be able to stop crying' which is supposed to happen three or four days after giving birth, but I don't seem to have had it until now. I've been so okay up until this point and shocked at how little I have cried. Maybe this is the day, maybe it's delayed for me because I had a caesarean or because of the iron levels, or because of the blood-pressure tablets. Who knows, but today I could cry at anything.

My midwife calls by this afternoon and officially discharges me from their care. My blood pressure has been stable for ten days straight, so there is no other reason for me to continue to be monitored daily. I know I've been really lucky to have daily visits for this long and have only had to go to the doctor to review the medication, which I must continue to do. The midwife's parting words to me are, 'You've got this, Canty' while she gives me a massive, comforting hug. Have I? I can't stop crying! She's reassuring and tells me a little baby blues is perfectly normal. Apparently, I'll feel differently when I'm off the drugs and have got through this initial newborn bit. I take her word for it and off she goes.

I message the antenatal girls to tell them I've been discharged but that I still feel a bit rubbish. They send sympathetic messages back and tell me they are there for me. I know they are. I'm so lucky be in a decent group who will share the truth and not just try to get one up on each other.

15TH JUNE

Our pals Holly and Chris are visiting from London so I'm busy on the internet looking at how we can entertain them. This is me; I like to have a plan and I always offer activities to visiting friends. Just because we have had a baby and sleep is not part of my life now, that is not going to change. I decide we should go to the local food festival as it looks like the rain will stay away until later in the afternoon and it's not far from our house.

They arrive and I feel really pleased to see them. Holly looks at me and asks if I'm okay. I think how much I love and miss her now we have moved away. We all go into the front room and Arthur starts crying so, cool as a cucumber,

I just start to feed him. Inside, I feel like I'm going to die of embarrassment, and I imagine the pair of them are feeling the same too. Yes, we have shared a lot of time together and we are all pretty close but how is it 'normal' to release the clasp on your bra to free your nipple in front of your friends, sober, in broad daylight and in your living room? Being British, I didn't want to be a stereotypical prude and go into another room – that would just make it weird, or has what I have done made it weird? I don't know and, after a while, Chris goes into the kitchen to help Rhys with tea. I feel sorry for him but relieved it's just me and Holly and my big white boob.

Rhys packs up the pram and my new, totally unstylish handbag/baby suitcase, and there is only one thing left to do – we have to leave the house and go to the festival, the planned activity.

As we start to walk down the road I feel it, a panic building deep in my chest. This is clearly evident on my face as Holly puts her arm around my waist, and I'm pleased she's there. That doesn't take away this growing feeling, though. I find I'm worried about where we'll sit to eat lunch so I suddenly suggest to everyone that we should maybe stop at a local café on the way. The boys question why we would do that when we are on our way to a food festival where there will be loads of food options and, not wanting to unleash the crazy or make myself sound totally incapable, I have no answer for this so we keep walking.

I can't understand why no one else thinks it's important to know where we'll sit so everyone is comfortable. But I guess I'm the one with the baby and therefore the only one who is incapable of 'going with the flow'.

As we get to the festival the heavens open. I'm standing in a park with a screaming 14-day-old baby who weighs not much more than a bag of sugar and there is, as predicted (!), nowhere for us to sit. For the first time I think, *I told you so*, and it's a phrase that becomes etched in my brain. From this day forward, I will regularly predict the worst-case scenario for me and Arthur, the thing that would make it all unbearable. And from this day forward, that scenario plays itself out again and again.

Today, all I can think about is that we're supposed to be entertaining our friends. We're supposed to be showing them how easy this baby thing is, how we're so all over it. But here I am, having a panic attack in the rain, struggling to get my breath while Arthur screams and I can see the panic in their faces. I tell them to go and get themselves some lunch and they do.

I manage to find some metal steps out the back of one of the vans. I perch there to try to peel off my many layers to get to Arthur's food source. It strikes me that this also isn't 'normal', having to strip down to your bare breast in the rain, in public. As soon as he's latched and I start to do some deep breathing, a door hits me on the back of the head.

'You can't sit here', a young woman informs me. I look at her, hoping she'll see that I have a tiny baby feeding from me. But she doesn't seem to care. She just repeats 'You can't sit here.'

I want to tell her that I hope when she has a baby one day someone will hit her on the back of the head with a door in the rain and tell her she can't feed the baby there. But I don't have the strength and I don't want to cry again so I get up and walk away.

Our friends reappear so Rhys goes to get us something to eat, which he feeds me while I'm feeding. We manage to find some plastic chairs to sit on, which actually belong to the champagne tent but it turns out they have more empathy than the van lady and let us sit there.

I just about get through the rest of the day. The sun finally comes out and everyone perks up.

Except me. My mood doesn't alter at all. Despite the seemingly trivial nature of the afternoon's events, deep inside I know that something has changed today. And the adrenaline has well and truly been used up.

This has not been right. I decide it's best to go out only if absolutely necessary from now on.

CHAPTER 2

THE DESCENT

19TH JUNE

Alison and Bernard are back from their second trip to see more of the UK and I'm relieved as Rhys is going to go back to work properly in the next few days and it will be good to have them around. I can't even imagine what it will be like to be on my own with a baby. Most of the antenatal class's other halves have gone back to work and they have mainly coped. Future Laura will have to cope but, right now, with Alison and Bernard in the house, Laura has an out.

20TH JUNE

It's 03:16. My teeth are chattering while I burp Arthur. He's puked his entire feed and as I feel it run down me, my teeth start chattering with the cold. In a bid to make sure I can get back to bed as soon as possible, I change him and feed him the rest of what my boobs have to offer and thank goodness his eyes are now closing. I'm not holding him close; I don't want to get him wet from the milk on me that I swear has seeped through to my pants. I tell myself I'm going to jig him around until I have counted to sixty and then I'll creep up the stairs and hope he settles. He does. I take off my feeding bra, massive pants and pyjamas and try to give myself a wash with his baby wipes. I debate an actual 3am shower but I don't want to wake either him or Rhys. I fumble in my chest of drawers to find clean, dry pants, a bra and PJs and pull stuff out that will do. I stink.

While lying there, I Google how I can stop my baby puking and send an SOS to the antenatal group. That's the wonder of the group: out of eight of us, you can pretty much guarantee that someone will reply to you no matter what time of day (or night). After about an hour, I settle on the fact that Arthur must see a cranial osteopath as soon as possible.

21ST JUNE

We manage to get an appointment with the osteopath this morning, after I cried on the phone and told her every last detail of his puking. She pulls him in all sorts of directions and I almost feel a bit sorry for him. Then he cries all the way home and pretty much most of the morning. I start texting the osteopath asking if this is normal and, of course, the answer is yes.

He finally goes down for a sleep after lunch, so I feel it's acceptable to tell Rhys I'm going to try to negotiate having some sleep myself. Of course, I tell him to wake me if Arthur wakes and is hungry.

I wish I could detach my breasts and leave them down here but that's not a thing. I know it's futile trying to sleep in the day, or at any time, and I hope that maybe one time I won't have to listen to the whole episode of *Blue Gold* narrated by Stephen Fry on my sleep-stories app before I can sleep for longer than ten minutes. As I start to go up the stairs, there is a knock on the door and a friend is here to visit with her newborn. Everything inside me sinks. I know I haven't replied to her messages. I know she doesn't care that I haven't and just wants to say hi and introduce her baby, but I feel all kinds of awkward. We have tea and chat but I'm not present.

I realise that I'd rather not see anyone. I didn't even pick up when my mum called today. I just don't have the energy.

22ND JUNE

I walk into the kitchen with the intention of making some lunch. The last few days, I've just had a piece of shortbread which a neighbour baked for us. Thank goodness she did, it's been the only real source of calories I've had between waking up and someone cooking for me in the evening. I don't seem to have the mental capacity to know how to put a sandwich together. And even if I do manage to make a sandwich, I will make a mess and there will be crumbs and then I'll have to tidy them up and how will I do that? Rhys doesn't come home for lunch today, so I just go without,

I can't take any more shortbread. I don't feel hungry, so this isn't a problem. There is nothing really in the fridge; I know it's my fault because I should be getting the food in.

I sit down to do an online food order but I don't know what we need. I don't know how to put a simple meal together, let alone think about what we need for the week. The panic inside me is at fever pitch while I look at the cursor flashing in the search bar.

Feeling the immense pressure to do the food shopping, but seemingly not being able to do it, is such a confusing and intense feeling. I keep telling myself that this is not a hard task. Why can I not do it? There is no real answer apart from perhaps a few wires have come a bit loose and that's why I can't think it through properly. I've been worried about what to order for days but I know I have to do it today as it's been over a week. I order things that I think will be useful but all I can think of is quiche. It's tasty, has good egg protein in it and we all don't mind it. I appear to be stockpiling quiche. We have quiche Lorraine filling the freezer, but I never get it out to have for lunch as then I'll have to replace it. I decide that today I shall have some to prove that I'm right for ordering it. But I must eat it straight out of the foil packet, so I don't dirty a plate and then have to clean it.

Is it worth cleaning one plate or should I wait for a few to build up? I don't want Alison to think I'm lazy. But which sponge should I use? There now appear to be a few around the sink, and I don't want to clean a plate with the floor sponge. I decide that in future if I'm eating by myself, I will only eat outside or straight out of the packaging or with a piece of kitchen roll in place of an actual plate. That makes much more sense.

I have lost the ability to make even the simplest decision. I have lost the ability to function like the human being I was the day before Arthur was born. I don't recognise this as something wrong with me; it's just the way it is. I am obsessed with mess and dirt and clutter, but I feel there is nothing I can do to remedy it. If I clean, it won't be good enough. I'm too lazy to move all the furniture, which I need to if I'm to do a good job. So, really, there is no point.

23RD JUNE

I lie in bed in a cold sweat. For some reason, I've remembered about a joint TSB account Rhys and I opened when we lived in London. I did the research, we went through the faff of opening it and then promptly ignored it.

All the bills were in my name and they came out of my account as I was the one who owned the house. Now that we live together, we *should* have added Rhys to the bills. We *should* have moved all the utility providers to the joint account, but I just haven't done it. I become obsessed that we've been charged for this account all along, even though it's not being used. Are we massively in debt? I lie in bed, sweating and panicking about this debt that may or may not exist. I can't move for thinking about it and hope that by lying really still it might just go away.

As soon as I go downstairs, I start talking to Alison about it. No 'Good morning', no niceties. I just spill what I have been worrying about for the last eight hours. She tells me that her name and her husband's are on all their bills and she has a filing cabinet in her study with all the relevant utilities slotted into the right place. Yes, of course you do, that's how proper adults live. I need to get a filing cabinet, I need to find all the right paperwork and I need to go and speak to someone at TSB as soon as it is open.

I tell Alison I'm going, and that's it, I'm off. I just take my purse, nothing else. It's a boiling hot day. I get to the bank and just look at the tellers. I'm the only customer there, which is just as well, because as soon as they look up, I start wibbling at them about being a new mum and not doing that well and needing to know if our account is overdrawn and if someone can tell me this, then I will know if I actually need to worry about it or if I can cross it off my worry list.

They look at each other. I know I am a mess and I am that crazy lady talking at them, but I don't care. I need to know.

One of them very kindly takes me into a side room and says she will help. She tells me to take a seat and her kindness means a tear pops onto my cheek. I quickly wipe it away but continue to softly sob. I can't sit still so I get up and start rocking like I am holding my baby.

An hour later, I find myself walking home in a daze. I feel okay about knowing we're not overdrawn and we have a whole £26 in the account. That worry can be ticked off but now I'm on to the immediate next one. The bills. There is no way of solving this…I don't know who provides us with what. I don't know where all the paperwork is apart from potentially in one of the piles of paperwork we have in the kitchen and on the little table in the dumping room. I can't remember any online passwords. They will need Rhys and I to be together to make the changes to the names on the bills. That almost never happens. This is the blocker I need. It would be better if I wasn't here, to stop messing things up.

I am a mess; our life is a complete mess.

24TH JUNE

It's Rhys's birthday today and I've been dreading it as I know we will have to leave the house. After a lot of debate (in my own head), I have booked a pub that is walking distance away. They are showing the World Cup, not that any of us is particularly interested but I have learned that all Australians will watch any sport if it's on and I'm going to lunch with three of them.

Rhys gets up in a good mood. We go downstairs and he opens presents my mum has left and the ones from me. So far so good. Rhys goes up to change Arthur as his mum and Bernard arrive. After doing a bit of small talk, I go upstairs to see why Arthur is screaming and to offer a boob but as I go into his room, I see exactly why he's in so much distress. Rhys has put him in a reusable nappy and is taking photos of his scrawny naked body in this massive red contraption.

The colour of the nappy clashes with his baggy newborn skin. The rage comes from my feet and I launch at him. 'Why are you doing this? I don't know how to use them! We don't have a system set up yet! We haven't talked about it! He obviously finds them uncomfortable!'

Rhys is shocked and tries to have a rational conversation with me but I'm not rational so everything in my head comes out in a jumble and I burst into tears. I go up to our room with my phone to unleash my anger in a WhatsApp stream of consciousness to Mum. She's saying all the right things, but I just don't want to hear it. I don't want today to be the day we try reusable nappies for the first time – we are going out and that is stressing me out enough as it is. Don't ask me why; eating out is something I would normally look forward to. Rhys comes up the stairs with a calmed-down Arthur in a cute outfit. 'Please don't ruin today for me,' he says. 'I'm sorry, I won't'. He kisses me on the cheek and they go downstairs. I take a few deep breaths and reread what Mum has sent.

I try my best to dress up. It's the first time I've been out since the disaster that was the food festival. I put on the same dress as I know it will fit and I don't want to go through the humiliation of trying to squeeze into anything else. Why does no one tell you that you need a temporary, perhaps four-week wardrobe after the birth when you don't want to be wearing maternity clothes as that makes you feel like shit but all the water and goo is still in your tummy so you can't get into your old clothes?

I go downstairs and as soon as I see Alison, I realise why Rhys had put Arthur in that reusable nappy. It was Alison and Bernard who brought us the reusable nappies, from Australia. I'm a terrible person. When we opened the gift when I was still pregnant, I thought it was a great idea. The designs were so cool. But hey, it seems I'm not that person any more and now change is the scariest thing anyone can impose on me.

Rhys packs the pram and we walk to the pub with Arthur in a disposable nappy. I try to do chat. I really do try, but I have nothing to say. My tummy is churning over and over. I'm not sure if it's guilt, hunger, fear...I feel like I'm vibrating and I'm not sure if they can hear me humming. We arrive and sit at the booked table, right next to another full table in a virtually empty pub. Annoying, but I realise it's under the TV as requested. We order. I don't fancy a roast so order a pasta dish. They don't have it. I order a salad as that's what a new mum should be eating to try to lose the baby weight. I poke the leaves around a bit to reveal defrosted avocado. Who actually freezes avocado? It obviously can't be done as it's more brown than green, like little slugs in my already unappealing salad.

Then Arthur needs feeding so I pick him up out of his pram and try to arrange a modesty feeding cloth over me. I can't settle him after his feed, he seems to want to cluster-feed in the middle of the day. This hasn't happened before and, of course, it is now happening in broad daylight. This is why we should never leave the house.

As the stress builds for all of us, Alison and Bernard say they have been talking and they want to offer Alison to stay for a bit to help us out. We're all now in tears, in the pub on Rhys' birthday, at the table next to the only other people in the pub. Rhys orders three gins. Good shout, for them. I'm desperate to go home and start looking at flights nearer Christmas for Alison, in the hope they will easily be able to transfer her ticket so that she can stay with us for a while.

Rhys smiles at me when we get home and says he's had a nice birthday. I know he's lying but I get a burst of love for him. *A birthday to forget* is what I know we are both thinking.

25TH JUNE

They haven't been able to transfer the flight. Today is the day they drive to the airport and I'm on my own. Today, more than the others, has a black cloud hanging over it. As we're all chatting in the kitchen, trying to pretend nothing bad is going to happen, Rhys asks me for a quiet word upstairs. He sits on the spare room bed, holds my hands and his open face smiles at me. What's he going to say?

He asks me what I think to us offering to pay for Alison's flight home to Australia.

Neither of us will be able to cope without help and we're just about to lose that. Money is on my worry list but I don't want to be on my own so there is no other answer. Rhys goes downstairs to negotiate with his mum and Bernard while I sit on the top step listening to their reaction. Poor them, I imagine they have got their heads around going on to Singapore and having a lovely, relaxing, not-having-to-look-after-anyone type holiday. Now we are asking if they will be apart, one to travel to Singapore on his own, the other to stay and live in our hell.

They agree. Of course. And with that, Bernard is unloading all of Alison's stuff into our spare room. I tiptoe around saying thank you and sorry repeatedly. Bernard has gone. One of the kindest men I know. I'm sad for Alison, so I force myself to try to be Enthusiastic Laura.

26TH JUNE

Dad's driving down again today. I feel I need to warn him what he's walking into, so I draft a text. What do I actually want to say? I'm not 100 per cent sure but I just want him to know that the Laura he saw the other week, fresh out of hospital and living the new-family dream, is no longer here. And I'm sorry, and I want to give him the opportunity to not come. Of course, he's coming and asks if there is anything he can do to help. I go through my worry list. The first one he can do is the blinds in Arthur's room.

The house was so close to finished when Arthur came. On Dad's first visit he couldn't believe how much we had done in a year and I need to remember that. Because I have been living with it being nearly finished for so long, I was just desperate for it to be complete for D-day. I reckon if Arthur had come on his due date, or late, 'like first babies usually are', then we would have been sorted and my worry levels might have been lower. I keep trying to remind myself that until not long ago, we were living between the kitchen and our room in the loft. The middle floor was a bomb site. At least Arthur's room was ready and at least I did the Ikea trip with Bernard and Alison so the living room is also temporarily done.

27TH JUNE

It's late afternoon as I come down from staring out of the window in our ensuite bathroom and I can hear eye-wateringly annoying American accents coming from the TV. It's about 27 degrees outside. As I've not been with them, acting like a drain, Rhys and Alison have decided they can squeeze in another episode of *Orange is the New Black*. It makes me so angry. They know that, but they do it anyway as they can't see anything wrong with it. And there is nothing wrong with it, but TV in the middle of the day, especially a hot day, has never been a thing for me unless I'm ill. It's a lovely, warm summer afternoon. We *should* be outside, we *should* be playing happy families, preparing dinner together while we coo over the new baby and sip wine like life is totally complete.

In the kitchen I look in the fridge again, but I don't know why. I still can't think how I could use any of its contents to make any kind of meal. It's 16:30 but it's now all on me to make some dinner by dinner time as they're just rotting away watching shit American drivel in the pokey, boiling hot, dirty front room. I don't know why I care about dinner as I'm never hungry, but that's what mums do, right? They provide for everyone, seamlessly, in the blink of an eye.

The need to be a productive and therefore a worthwhile human is overwhelming. So instead of just staring into the fridge, alone in the kitchen, I suddenly decide to epilate my legs and mop the floors. I give my legs about five minutes each and don't bother to moisturise them and then I start mopping the hallway floor right outside the front room. They tell me to stop and that they'll clean when the episode is finished. My blood is boiling. I hate them. I just want us to be together playing happy families. I don't want to be alone, but I don't want to watch the TV. I can't sit still, I don't have any idea what's going on in the show and I simply can't do TV in the day when it's hot outside, I just can't.

As well as trying to get them off the sofa and in the kitchen with me, I want to feel pleased with myself for managing to clean the floor and look after my unwieldy leg hair, but I don't get these feelings. All I can think is that the floor still looks dirty and I can still feel stubble on my now dry, flaking legs. I'm a failure at this, too. I don't know why I bother.

I text Mum telling her I just want to walk out of the door. She convinces me to go and tell Rhys how I feel and what I would like help with. I put the phone down and walk into the living room. I ask them if they can come and help me make some dinner and chat to me please. They don't reply, it's obviously a crucial bit. Rhys presses pause, reluctantly looks at me and says they will be through in a minute. I walk back into the kitchen and text Mum to tell her I've done it. She's pleased for me.

When they come into the kitchen, Rhys makes them both a gin and tonic and they sit in silence at the bench waiting for me to start the fun. This is not what I planned. I wanted them to bring the fun atmosphere, I wanted us all to talk happily about how great the weather has been and our days. But actually, we've all had rubbish days. I want to tell them to go back and continue watching as I can't think of anything to say but I don't want to be alone.

I get some random bits out of the fridge, dump them on the side and go and sit at the kitchen table to text Mum and tell her I've done the wrong thing and they hate me even more.

28TH JUNE

Last night was a typical night. I feel like I've not had a second of sleep and have been worrying about seeing the osteopath today. I'm pretty sure everyone thinks it's a waste of time but 'if it makes you feel better, go for it'. I don't know if it does or not and I can't make decisions. The easiest thing to do is cancel as then I won't have to leave the house. It gets to 08:00, I send the cancellation text with my apologies and don't look at my phone for the rest of the day.

Most nights, the mantra *this is hell…this is hell* floats across my brain and tonight is no different. I repeat it as I lie in bed, maybe out loud, angry at my body for not being asleep. I'm so exhausted but I just can't switch off. I feel like my whole body is vibrating like something that's malfunctioned and come slightly out of place, so now nothing is aligned and it's thrown everything out of whack. All my fellow mum pals tell me how tired they are and seem to sleep as soon as they get into bed, but I just can't. I've tried to make the room as dark and cool as possible but it's the middle of a good summer and all I can hear are the blinds gently banging on the windowsill as I've opened the windows just to the right width that any moving air is funnelled in. I can't be bothered to get up and do anything about it.

Maybe I have over-egged all the going-to-sleep things and now trying to get to sleep has become a thing so big in my head that it cannot be scaled. I try not to think about it but, obviously, the more I try not to think about it, the more it's all I can think about. I sprayed the lavender mist, I put lavender drops on my wrists, I've washed my feet so the blood in them now feels cool – top mum advice. (She also believes you swell when you go on holiday abroad so you should always take clothes that are slightly bigger than your size at home. It's nothing to do with the constant drinking and ice cream. I love her and her theories.) I've listened to a sleep story from beginning to end and I've read a couple of chapters of my book. I have done everything and nothing has worked.

Its 19:00 and I keep calculating how many hours I could sleep if Arthur wakes at 23:00. Every hour that goes by, I can't just delete one from my total, I have to recalculate as my head can't retain anything. I get angrier at every hour lost. Three hours pass with me being a tense, vibrating ball until Rhys comes to bed with a sleeping Arthur in his arms. I immediately say to him, 'I can't sleep, I haven't slept' and he asks me why as he places Arthur gently in his crib and goes to brush his teeth. *I can't sleep as I appear to be vibrating and my mind feels like it's popped out of my head and is running laps around the bedroom* is what I think, but don't vocalise it. I should have taken Arthur to the osteopath. As Rhys quietly slides into bed, I ask when Art was last fed, how much he's had and if he puked any of it. He just tells me to shhh which I know is the right answer but now, if it's possible, I'm even more angry as I can't try to predict when I'll be up. Not that this matters as I don't sleep. I'm the incredible non-sleeping woman. After about ten seconds, I hear Rhys's breath go from awake breathing to heavy, just-gone-to-sleep breathing and I wonder how many other mothers have had murderous thoughts towards their partners as they effortlessly and immediately fall asleep.

The only part of the day I'm alone with Arthur is right now, at night, while Rhys and everyone else are getting their eight hours. That's when there's no one around telling me how lucky I am, how cute he is, how happy I must be, so I have to try to do all of that for myself.

I hear him make a noise. I've not been asleep. How could I sleep when my brain won't turn off? I've been worrying about how I'll get to pregnancy yoga now that the one-way system has been rerouted, about what to order on the weekly shop. I worry that we can't afford to finish doing our house up, that we're the embarrassment of the street. I worry about things that need to be worried about and things that don't, but I can't help it.

His noises escalate so I get up and feel the familiar stabbing pain in the abdomen of someone who's just been cut open so a baby could be pulled out. I pick him up without looking at him. I don't want to know what he looks like; I'm scared of him and he's ruining my life. I don't know whether to change his nappy first or feed him. I have to make this decision on my own multiple times a night and the thinking about what I should do really hurts.

As I'm changing his nappy, I repeat in my head, *I don't want this. How could anyone want this?* Life with a kid is miserable, and no one in their right mind could want that. I don't want it either, but I have it.

I sit down to feed him on what is rapidly becoming my least favourite sofa. I go for the right boob as the thought of him latching onto the painful, scabby nipple on the other side makes me feel like I'm going to vomit. As I'm feeding him, I check in with my antenatal group on WhatsApp. It's standard stuff – they're all crying for help, asking questions, trying new things and recommending them or not. We're all first-time mums, but we all ask each other's opinions on how to do everything. What a rubbish audience to ask baby-related questions to. None of us has been here before and none of us knows what we're doing. It's like the blind leading the blind but I guess there is some comfort in feeling like you can answer someone's question, regardless of what you say.

I keep trying to think of Arthur growing up with his cousin, my twin brother's son. I imagine them riding their bikes together and my sister-in-law and me laughing about those nights when we didn't get any sleep. I think about how he'll learn all sorts of boy things, the things Rhys did as a child with his father. I repeat these thoughts around and around in my head like I do every night, trying to give myself hope that I just have to get through this bit. This time will pass.

But very quickly the forced happy thoughts can't be forced any more, they are just pushed to the back of my mind by everything else. The noise won't stop. What am I going to do?

And then, everything comes together, all the musings in my brain, and I have a eureka moment.

The only way I can make it stop is to be dead. I need to die.

I can't think how, or when, but all of a sudden I'm excited that I have realised what the answer is. I feel slightly terrified at the thought of how I'll get from living to dead when I'm only 37, and apart from a slowly healing abdomen and high blood pressure, I'm fit and healthy. I'm not naturally at death's door. So, I'll have to get there some other way…

Ah! I realise I'm having a suicidal thought; they do exist and I'm having one. Well, there you go, it is possible, and I can totally see how people get there when I have never, ever considered anything like this before. But it's so exhilarating and it feels so right. I stand at Arthur's bedroom window gently patting his back, debating with myself if I think it's high enough or not. Maybe the ensuite window upstairs would be better?

I sit down again and think about the knife drawer downstairs and how I could take a knife out. Then, where I would cut. I think about how I could do it quickly and painlessly. I think of how hard I'll have to press into my wrists to cut the arteries. I wonder how it will feel as all the red blood just runs out of me. I know I'll feel its warmth, but will it hurt, or will I just slowly fall into a peaceful sleep, never to wake again? That's the dream. And it's the most positive and excited I've felt for a good while. This could really happen. This could be a plan.

Arthur would be far better off with someone else as a mum. All my friends seem to like him, and my family and even the midwife think he's cute (I guess she says that to everyone). They would all make way better mums than me and they wouldn't have to go through the whole awful, long drawn-out pregnancy stage. I've had a pretty cute, healthy one and he's all ready to go. Rhys loves him so he'll look after him too, he'll always have a dad, that's fine.

And then another thought.

As I'm changing his nappy it suddenly comes to me that maybe it's not me that has to be dead. Perhaps Arthur will just die of something while on Rhys's watch – then it wouldn't be my fault. We'd eventually get over the loss and we could then start living how we used to, right? Or perhaps I could kill Arthur and then go to prison. At least then I wouldn't have to live with a baby. I'd do my time and then I'd get out and then we could just continue living our lives like we did before, without a baby, bliss.

But then how would I hurt Arthur enough to kill him? I couldn't do that. So, I don't know how it will happen, but I know that I've found the solution and it is definitely for one of us to be dead.

I walk back up the stairs to our room, safe in the knowledge that this will end. As I lay Arthur asleep in his crib, go to the loo, have a sip of water, take some painkillers and get into bed, I realise that I have cracked it, I no longer feel anything like as crazed as I did earlier today. Or as confused as I have done for weeks. That's it.

I fall straight into a deep, deep sleep.

I have the answer to all my questions.

I have managed to silence my mind.

29TH JUNE

Ellie pops round, casually, to see us, me. I realise it must be a Saturday. Or a Sunday. I love her but today I don't want her to be here. I want to be all alone, under the sheet on my bed thinking through how I'll actually do it.

I try to make small talk, as does she, but she knows me too well. She asks if I want to go for a walk.

I don't.

Rhys thinks I should go and so does his mum. I guess I have to.

She asks me where I want to go. I don't know. I feel total dread for leaving the house.

The dread in my head is obvious as my physical body is shaking. We walk towards the front door and as Ellie looks back to ask if I'm all right, she has a kind, sympathetic smile on her face. I want her to be bored of me being so miserable, I want her to shout at me, I want her to hate me so she won't care when I'm found dead.

How could anyone miss this dribbling excuse for a mum? Ellie would be a great mum. It's so evident how much she loves Arthur, this would be a perfect solution. Her and Rhys could be like the odd couple bringing up a baby together, I'm sure they would be fine with that.

We step out, the sun is so bright it hurts my eyes. I go back inside and spend as long as I can looking for sunglasses. Ellie has the patience of a saint and when we finally make it out of the house, we turn left and find ourselves in the park. It's the park we normally walk Alma in, so I automatically start walking laps. After about a quarter of a lap, I find myself telling Ellie everything. And I finally get to the bit about needing to die.

'Okay…' says Ellie, reacting calmly. 'Have you mentioned this to the doctor at all?'

'No, not yet, but I have an appointment about my blood pressure this afternoon so if there's time, I'll mention it then.'

'There will be time,' she says confidently. 'I think you really need to. They need to know exactly how you are feeling. Is Rhys going with you?' she asks.

'I know, I know', I say dismissively. 'I'm going with Alison.'

I feel incredibly nervous and panicky. It's one thing telling a best friend but how can I tell a stranger? They don't know me and what I'm like, they will assume I'm a terrible person. How could anyone want to leave their tiny baby with no mummy? I *am* a terrible person, they would be 100 per cent right to think that.

I don't know how many laps we have completed and how many miles we have walked but as we are ticking them off, I realise I don't want to go back home. Home feels like a prison, the place where I am tied to the small child. Out here in the Alma park with my pal, I feel so free. Apart from the subject matter, this could be like any day Ellie and I have had together waffling away, her being sensible and practical, me spouting an unconscious stream of what's in my head and her just getting it. But Ellie needs to get on with her day and Arthur will need feeding soon, I'm sure, so she walks me home.

There's no way I could tell Rhys how I'm feeling so it feels kind of good to tell Ellie. I'm not sure why, but the feeling I have inside me is like the one I had last night, one of contentment. Rhys is working so hard, holding together his business while still trying to finish our house, entertain his visiting mother and look after Arthur and me. I can't possibly tell him how dark my thoughts are, as I know how much he loves Arthur and I know how much we all really wanted to enjoy being with his family who have flown half way around the world to share this exciting time with us. Telling them I want to die would really bring the mood down. Rhys loves his son more than I think he can believe, and I can't make this experience even worse for him. I also don't want to reveal what a truly horrid person I am to the man I love. He wouldn't want to marry me if I told him I wanted to kill myself or Arthur. That I know for certain.

Alison walks with me to the doctor. When I'm called in, she waits in the waiting room with Art and I vibrate my way to the doctor's office. I'm sweating. She takes my blood pressure and surprisingly it's okay. I can come off the tablets. This is good news and I quickly remember what the midwife said. 'You are Laura on Labetalol – once you come off it, you'll feel different.' The doctor asks how I've been feeling in myself and, with the Labetalol thought in my head, I downplay last night's feelings. I tell her I'm not feeling great, followed by all the excuses why. She listens patiently, suggests I have a bit of mild postnatal depression and gives me a card with the name of an NHS counselling service on it. I thank her and make a quick exit.

In the waiting room, Alison is jigging about with a crying Arthur; she's sweating also but is calm, my nirvana. I immediately feel guilty for letting my baby starve. I move the chair to face the wall and feed him, trying to breathe and think cool thoughts. I can see a visible sweat patch growing on my top from underneath where I'm holding him. How very disgusting. He eventually finishes and I put him on my shoulder to burp him, praying that he won't vomit in the waiting room. I turn around to aim him at the wall so his puke doesn't hit anyone. This leaves me facing the room. I can't look up. I just stare at my feet and gently pat him. Alison gets eye contact with me and kindly offers to take everything out so I can just walk outside into the relative cool with Arthur on my shoulder. I take her up on the offer and we walk home pretty much in silence. She gets it.

30ᵀᴴ JUNE

I open the door to Lydia. She's come all the way from London to see us. I know she loves babies, but I can't believe she'd want to give up a day and spend four hours on a train to come to our hell. I watch her with my scrawny baby; she thinks he's beautiful. He's not, I know that, but I guess it's what people say. She and Alison are chatting, but I can't think of anything to say that's not baby-related now I've asked her all about life in the outside world. I'm envious of her life and her tales. My mind is running in overdrive, thinking about how much Lydia loves babies and I know she wants to have a family. She could have this one. While we are in the kitchen alone, I see my opportunity. 'Take him back to London with you, Lyds.' She thinks I'm joking. I know she can't, but still, I have hope and this could be a possible perfect solution for when I go through with it.

After trying to nap for an hour and failing, I come downstairs to find the house empty. Have they gone to London with him? Are they working things out? I feel nothing inside. My boobs are throbbing.

I'm in the hallway motionless…

I don't know how long I've been here, but they eventually return, with Arthur. They have been out for a walk and to the shops. How very lovely. Look how easy it is for the pair of them. He really does need to be with Lydia, she's perfect.

As I feed him, we discuss how much I hate breastfeeding but I know it's what's expected and I know I'm lucky I can do it, blah, blah, blah. There is a big, black block in my head that will not allow me to learn how to bottle-feed. It's not just a case of shove it in their mouth, I'm pretty sure of that. There is sterilisation involved and I have never done that before. Lydia suggests talking about the pros and cons. She's a business consultant, like me. We like order, we like plans, we like a reasoned argument and we like black and white. Good idea, Lyds, well done, my brain appears to have forgotten how to be rational, and you've woken that part of me up. Good work! I think an hour passes before I'm persuaded (by the cold hard facts we have amassed) and we are agreed that we should introduce a bottle at night.

Rhys is on the same page and says he will pick up what we need on his way home from work. I have made a decision, based on something sensible, and we are going to change something that will make it better. I don't know how it will happen or how we will achieve this, but a bubble of enthusiasm rises in me at the thought of not having to be disturbed every ninety minutes. Thank goodness Lydia came. I know I wouldn't have been able to make this decision without her facilitation. I hope she doesn't charge me.

As Rhys comes to bed, I'm still awake and ask how Arthur took the bottle. I might as well have stayed up and fed him, I've not been asleep. Apparently, he took it like a pro. I could have been sleeping for four whole hours if I could just silence my head.

1ST JULY

Bec calls and asks if I want to go for coffee. This is a normal, lovely thing to do with a friend on a weekend. But of course, Ellie must have told her about our conversation. It's okay, I say, we're just going to have a quiet one.

I don't want to see her, I don't want to spend time with her, I don't want her to get too attached to me, as I won't be here for long. I don't even know if I like coffee any more, but I realise that's not the point. She comes over regardless and I realise how good it is to see her smiling face. She asks if I want to go out or if she should put the kettle on. I don't know. I've lost all ability to make any kind of decision, no matter how big or small. She tells me to put my shoes on so we can go out. But I can't go out as I haven't brushed my teeth and they're really yellow. She tells me to pop upstairs and brush them while she finds me some shoes. Why do my friends have to be so frustratingly kind and caring? I swear they're just trying to make things harder for me. Is what I told Ellie really that shocking? I don't really know any more.

We wander down to Bath Road and into the only coffee shop open at this time on a Sunday. I can hear her ordering a skinny cappuccino and a piece of carrot cake – I love her, she knows me so well. She comes back to our table and I ask how she is. She doesn't answer, she just wants to know how I am. I tell her I still hate it, motherhood, and ask her a million questions about what she did when her baby was tiny and hope that one of the answers is that she went away for six weeks while someone else reared him. I can't be the only person who finds this whole experience so utterly frustrating, exhausting, hopeless. She answers with what I know is the truth: she just kept going, doing what she had to do and now she has a fully functioning two-year-old. *Everyone else* can do it, *everyone else* gets through it, *everyone else* enjoys it, *everyone just gets on with it*. It's just me who's lazy and can't be arsed to look after my own baby.

We wander home. I don't want to as I know the baby is there, but I know I have to as the baby is there, so that's what we do. As we pass the corner with the church on, I tell her calmly that I can't go on.

To my shock, she breaks down – in big ugly sobs.

I feel bemused, but I guess this has been the elephant in the room the whole time and it's been building to this moment.

She tells me in the firmest voice I've ever heard from her: 'You'd better not do anything stupid, Laura'.

This surprises me. Bec has loads of friends and they're all functioning and not a drain. I thought this news would be music to her ears. Apparently not.

Bec holds my head, looks into my eyes and repeats, 'You'd better not do anything stupid, Laura. Promise me!'

I'm shocked and I'm embarrassed and it hits home.

I don't want to upset her, I love her. She's the best. I tell her that I saw the doctor yesterday and mentioned how I was feeling. I also tell her about the number I have to ring. Her hands move from the sides of my head to embrace me. We stand there, in the passageway next to the church with tears rolling down our faces. I don't care who sees us, I don't care who walks past. All I care about this minute is comforting Bec and trying to take away the hurt I have selfishly caused her.

After I don't know how long, it seems right to walk back home. I hang my head in shame the whole way, knowing deep down that I still want to die – but now I need to work out how I do that without hurting Bec.

2ND JULY

I find that every fourth night I must be so overly exhausted that I do actually sleep for a bit before my body forces me awake. I roll over to find Rhys isn't in bed and Arthur isn't in his cot. I feel so disappointed that I probably haven't slept for very long if they are still downstairs. I click my phone to see what time it is, knowing this is the worst thing you can do if you want to go back to sleep, but I need to know. Its 01:30 in the morning. I'm convinced something bad has happened, but I feel pleased and relieved. Maybe Rhys has fallen asleep downstairs and Arthur has hurt himself or perhaps he's choked on his last bottle and they have had to go to hospital…loads of scenarios play out in my head.

I lie there feeling devastated and relieved at the same time. I don't know what to do and I don't want to find a dead body, so I don't go downstairs to check if any of my scenarios are the truth. Instead, I pull the sheet up higher and hope that I can sleep for eight hours and everything will be okay in the morning.

While I'm under the covers, I start gouging away at the crust inside my nose. One thing I get a sense of achievement from is picking my nose. I absolutely love it and every time I go in, I want to bring bigger and bigger pieces out. Like I'm picking away at my head, my thoughts, ripping pieces of my stupid brain out, bit by bit. It started as a guilty pleasure under the cover of darkness and when feeding at night, once I'd replied to all my WhatsApp messages, Googled everything there is to Google and no one else seemed to be awake. It then migrated to a mandatory activity while I was on the loo. Trips to the toilet took ages as nothing could be 'forced' so once I'd done everything I could think to do on my phone, I'd start picking. The more I pick, the more there is to pick as the bits that had been picked the day before would have scabbed over. The bigger the bit that comes out, the more satisfaction I get.

If there is no tissue nearby, I just wipe it on my leg and if I remember to brush it off into a bin when it has dried then fine – if not, I don't care; it blends in with my gross appearance perfectly. Mum bun, baby puke down my back, snot on my leg. How is this okay, Laura? This is something that you stare at drivers for doing on their way to work and give them a 'shame on you' type look. But I don't care. It gives me a few minutes where my brain is occupied with thinking about digging into my poor nostrils and not about everything that is worrying me. I eventually stop caring about who sees me and start to practise my new hobby in broad daylight in front of anyone who happens to be there.

I don't want to do a Daniella Westbrook (Google her and her nose and I'm sure you'll stare at the photos for a long time) but I just can't help it. Rhys and his mum start calling me out for it and they are right. The inside of my nose is so sore, red raw and painful. I ask Ellie to get me some Savlon, which I force myself to snort every night to stop it going crusty and tempting me to pick. But none of this makes much difference. I can't stop myself.

3RD JULY

Its Ellie's birthday but we spend most of our meet-up talking about me, obviously.

When she asks me about my visit to the doctor, I admit I didn't mention the 'S' word and she does her disappointed face. I know that face and I want to make it go away. I resolve to call the doctor as soon as we go home. I promise her.

I'm fourth in the queue so I hang up. I pace around for the rest of the morning, waiting for Rhys to come home for lunch. As soon as he does, I tell him Ellie thinks I need to go back to the doctor, and I think she's right. He dials and we're second in the queue. When the receptionist asks me what the appointment is regarding, I can't get my words out. I'm sobbing and feel so panicked about the news going outside of my close circle. Rhys takes over booking the appointment while holding me, so I don't start having a full-on panic attack. He hangs up and says we are going the day after tomorrow to see Dr Cox at 11:00, he'll come home and pick us up at a quarter to. That's it, we're going and I have to tell this doctor, this time. I'm scared of what will happen if I don't.

4TH JULY

It's my mum's 70th birthday today. I'm such a terrible person. I have not sent flowers; I've not even called her. I have ordered a present for her which has arrived at our house but I have failed to put it in the post to her. Every day I have looked at it on the side and thought Future Laura will take that to the post office. That would not have been so difficult to do but I just haven't been bothered the last few days and now Future Laura is here and she feels crap. I should know by now that leaving things to Future Laura will always backfire.

I spend most of the day worrying about what I'm going to say to the doctor and predicting how she will react. There is no other way for her to react in my mind:

'You are a lazy mother. Go home. Buck your ideas up and start looking after your beautiful baby boy!'

And that would be me told.

CHAPTER 3

THE DIAGNOSIS

5TH JULY

Rhys comes to get us just before 11:00, when my anxiety about missing the appointment has manifested into repeatedly opening and closing the front door and looking up the doctor's number on my mobile. When we get there, we are seen right away. I'm immediately relieved to see the doctor is one I recognise and not fresh out of medical school. Not that there is anything wrong with that and everyone needs to start somewhere, but I need one capable of reading between the lines and I guess it takes experience to be able to do that.

We sit down together while Arthur sleeps in his pram.

The doctor asks me that common question that I don't think has an answer: 'Now, how can I help?' I tell her I've been very anxious, and I've not been able to sleep. The more she questions, the more just spills out of my mouth, no reading between the lines required. I keep looking at Rhys when I get stuck and he just nods, reassuring me it's okay to carry on. He continues to rub my shoulder with the arm that's wrapped around me.

Ellie and Bec's faces are firmly in my mind, as well as their parting words, 'You must tell the doctor everything', and 'You'd better not do anything stupid'. The doctor does not look shocked, she just has her sympathetic head on (slightly to one side, slight smile, nod). I think this is when I know she's not going to tell me to suck it up. I feel all kinds of bubbles in my tummy, like there is a wind-up toy running around and around my insides. Tears start to flow down my face as soon as I answer yes to the 'have I thought about ending my life?' question. I can't believe I'm nodding, affirmative. I look at Rhys, acknowledging it's news to him. He doesn't say anything, he has the same smile on his face. I'm worried about what he's actually thinking.

Does he think he's marrying a monster? Does he think I'm lazy too and I'm just saying this as I just want someone to do the work for me?

The doctor has heard enough and quickly wraps up the dialogue. I'm so distressed, I can barely breathe but I think I'm actually relieved that I have told someone medical and she has acknowledged it as a problem and not told me I'm lazy. This doesn't change the fact that I think I'm lazy, of course.

I notice Arthur is in Rhys's arms and starting to make 'I'm hungry' noises. The doctor says very decisively, 'We can help you, you will get through this', while looking right at me. 'Go home and someone from the Crisis Team will call you.' I suck the dribble back in that has evidently escaped while I have been hanging on the doctor's every word. And we thank her, very much.

I wonder what on earth Rhys is thinking.

From the moment we leave the doctor's office I feel like a massive wave of NHS goodness has just hit me. They know, they will help, everything will be okay, and I've got away with being useless again.

Rhys doesn't say much on the drive home, apart from the practicalities of him going back to work and checking I'll be okay with his mum at home. I agree. The fact that I want him by my side every minute of every hour of every day, I realise, is typically selfish of me.

Just as the doctor has said, my phone starts ringing about 15 minutes after we get home. A quietly spoken lady introduces herself as being from the Crisis Team. *A questionable name for a mental-health team* is my first thought, but there you go, it does what it says on the tin, I guess. She asks me all the same questions I had been asked in the doctor's surgery and I blub my way through telling her exactly how I feel. A theme with everyone I speak to from now on is that they all tell me they will help and I will get better, but I just cannot see it happening. It's all right saying it but it's not the actual truth, is it? I'm relieved to be in 'the system' but I just can't see *how* anyone will help me. They keep saying they will, so I just have to hope.

The conversation ends with her asking me if I can keep myself safe. What? Safe from what? Oh, from me? Wow, this is serious, I am well and truly in the system. I stand up from the spare bed where I've found myself and wander up into our bedroom. My mind starts thinking of this nanny the NHS will provide, that must be what they mean when they say they are going to help. It's the only thing that will actually help, that or give Arthur to someone who wants him, and I imagine that process will take a lot longer. I think about how she will turn up at the door with a big grin on her face as she tells me I don't need to worry, and she will make things all better. And then I snap out of it, telling myself I'm an idiot for thinking such ridiculous things.

A few hours later, as advised, two young nurses appear at the door. They ask me everything again. I have already been asked everything twice! I'm now more angry than tearful and tell the story with far less detail. I'm conscious that I don't want to come across as a terrible, ungrateful person but I can't understand why they are wanting me to say those words again. They both look knackered and I'm sure, given the choice, they would rather not be squashed onto a tiny sofa in a sweleringly hot living room with a crying stranger, her husband and her mother-in-law. They listen through bleary eyes (how long have these kids been on shift?) and then one of them bends down to get something out of her bag. A teeny, weeny, fold-up nanny perhaps?

I see it's a very small white box with a sticker on. She looks down at the box and asks if I want some drugs to help take away the anxiety. What a stupid question, does the pope shit in the woods? The magic pill that will take me from this hyper state to normal again – *thank goodness* is what I think. I look at Rhys and with a big grin on my face say, 'Yes, please' and take the box that's offered. Thank you. I want to hug them, but I don't think it's appropriate, so I lean into Rhys instead. As they go on their way, I really hope home to their beds, I'm relieved I'm going to have the best night's sleep I've had in a long time. There is just the small matter of getting the baby fed. We agree Rhys will wait up and do the last feed as late possible in the hope that I won't be disturbed for as long as possible.

I go off to bed at 19:30, straight after dinner, safe in the knowledge I won't be disturbed as Rhys and Alison will do the last bottle. The firm hope, and I guess the belief, is that I will sleep and wake up many hours later, less of a shaking, lazy mess.

The blazing sun is still high in the sky and the temperature reads 31 degrees in our bedroom. I start the bedtime routine and climb in. The next thing I know I'm on a really large boat and then, all of a sudden, I realise I'm in our bedroom, in bed, sat up feeling my pillow and it is dripping wet. I can't work out what's reality and what is a dream. I come to the conclusion that the only thing that could have made my pillow that wet is dribble and that I've been so drugged and in such a deep sleep that I've managed to dribble my pillow sopping wet. I stumble down the stairs with Arthur to feed him in his room. On the sofa where all of the thinking seems to happen. I try to be positive, thinking about when Arthur is older and can run around, playing with his cousin. But then Arthur vomits the milk he's just drunk, and my thoughts very quickly switch back to the solution, and the method.

My life is just sloppy poo, watery vomit and next to no sleep.

Seriously, who wants this?

6TH JULY

Today is Alma's lady operation which I remember booking when I was pregnant and delighting in telling the receptionist that I would be a mum next time they saw me. Rhys takes Alma; I feel sorry for her, but I know it's a necessary evil. The last thing I want is another load of babies in the house, even if they would be cute and furry.

Soon after he leaves, there is a knock on the door. It's two ladies, they are from the Crisis Team again. One declares herself as scared of dogs the instant I open the door. I have no patience for this but she's in luck this time with Alma being under the knife.

We sit in the lounge while Alison stays with Arthur in the kitchen. They have come to see how last night went. I tell them that the pill worked a treat until Arthur woke and I fed him in the early hours. They seem surprised and ask why Rhys wasn't able to. I explain that I have always fed in the night as Rhys is back at work and I'm still breastfeeding. I explain that we had only recently introduced that one bottle to try to help me get a bit of sleep early evening. They look at each other, a tad embarrassed. They have come with more of those drugs in case they worked, and I wanted to use them for another couple of nights, but I can't have them if I am getting up in the night to feed. I should never have had them. Furthermore, they realise that I go down a flight of stairs to feed Arthur in the night and they can't believe I managed it. I think of the amount of paperwork they will have to fill in when they get back to the office and how they will have to change or update a load of policy documentation to include 'you must confirm if the mother is still breastfeeding through the night before prescribing...' Poor them. And stupid me for disclosing. I realise now I'm looking at another sleepless night.

7TH JULY

Alison and I are in the lounge watching Wimbledon when Rhys gets home from work. Alma's on the rug near my feet and Rhys bends down to look at her wound. I hear Alma whimper and I see that Rhys is touching the wound gently. I don't know if you have ever heard a dog whimper but it's one of the saddest, most heart-wrenching noises you will EVER hear. As Rhys lifts her, Alma makes an even louder whimper and before we realise what's happened there is wound juice spraying out of her tummy and onto the rug. I look around the room and notice we all have our mouths wide open. We have just witnessed *Alien*, the live show, in our own living room on our own dog.

Rhys rushes to the car with Alma in his arms and Alison gets in the passenger side, shouting for more towels. Before I realise what has actually happened, they are racing to the vet and I'm in the lounge on my own, standing in what appears to be a crime scene. In that moment, I feel utter despair.

The lounge is now RUINED, our dog is going to die, Rhys is going to be even more upset than he already is, what on earth is the point of living? This is the absolute final sign to me that I need to tap out. I think it's the very first time I have been left on my own with Arthur. I notice he's still asleep, so I go to the kitchen and look under the sink. What to use as blood and goo remover is not obvious. I go for generic kitchen cleaner and a sponge. I start to gently dab at the blood and then think *fuck it* and start to scrub at it. After about twenty minutes and for the first time in a long time, I take a look at the rug and think I've actually done a pretty good job. I'm looking forward to showing Rhys and Alison.

About an hour later and with Arthur sleeping the whole time, I'm relieved to see the car pulling into the drive so rush to the front door. I see Alma is in Rhys's arms and as I open the door to greet them, Alma's stomach bursts open again and there is now wound juice all over the concrete steps. So off they go again, no words spoken between the three of us, just more, utter disbelief. I didn't have time to show them the clean rug and now I have blood on one of the only three pairs of bottoms that fit me.

When they return, they are both pale and look exhausted. I'm disappointed that they didn't notice my excellent cleaning job. Alma has a bandage right around her middle and has to go back in first thing for another operation. Rhys is insistent that he will sleep in the kitchen in her bed with her tonight. I know he will, he loves this dog and she has just been promoted to most critical in this house.

And so, this is the first night I'm alone in our bed at home since Arthur was born.

I have no idea why, but I still take him downstairs to his empty room to feed him in the night – I guess force of habit.

The Crisis Team are coming again tomorrow. I wonder what they will say and if they will come with a magic pill that's breastfeeding-friendly and only works for the amount of time before the first feed. Surely something like that must exist…

8TH JULY

Today is Ellie's birthday party. It's at her house and she's invited friends and their little ones for a lunchtime barbecue. I keep telling myself it will be okay because it just has to be. I know everyone, everyone is kind, and everyone will want to meet Arthur. And I guess that's the problem. I don't want them to coo at Arthur as it makes me mad that I don't have those feelings.

As soon as we go through the door, Rhys is like an animal being released into the wild. There are boys, there is beer, there is sunshine, this is 100 per cent his jam. That's the last I see of him for about two hours. I can't remember the last time he would have had fun and I'm really jealous of him having a good time. I feel nothing but panic.

One of the girls offers to look after Arthur after his cluster-feeding marathon is over, professing they miss theirs being that little. I don't know how I feel so I just hand him over and tentatively go and join the group sat around the table with all the food. I spot Rhys in the garden and realise this is the first time in a long time I have seen him do a proper, genuine smile. I berate myself over and over for not being able to relax and just have a good time. *There is nothing and no one here you do not like so just get on with it, be happy and have a good time.* But I remain joyless inside.

I give it about twenty minutes and the guilt of leaving Arthur with Ellie's friends is too much. They tell me they have changed his nappy and how cute and small it was compared to their child's. I just want to cry. Why do they find it so easy and everything petrifies me? I thank them and just want to get home. When I think about being at home, I realise I need to stay.

As we leave, the remaining few tell me I'm doing a great job. I can't take it; I give them a panicked stare and get in the car.

9TH JULY

The Crisis Team visit today and I notice it's one of the same ladies who has been before. She seems like she really wants to help but she just doesn't know how. They don't bring any pills today, which I am disappointed about. They know the health visitor is coming tomorrow so they'll come the day after. I'm not sure why.

10TH JULY

I'm feeding Arthur when the health visitor arrives. She asks me about the position I'm in and tells me a couple of different ways to hold him. Then she tells me how I could latch him differently, and about suck rhythms and fore and hind milk. Why is she doing this to me? Why would I want more ways to do something? More things to feel guilty about not trying, more things to learn. Is she hoping that the more ways I think I can do something, one of them will eventually stick? I'm angry but I nod and smile politely, saying I'll experiment a bit, knowing full well I'll keep doing what I'm doing as it's going okay for now. I pop new holds, new ways of feeding and the fact he needs to get to my 'hind milk' every time he feeds on my worry list all without moving a muscle and with a fixed smile on my face.

She asks me how I'm finding getting things done around the house and I tell her I'm basically not, all I do is feed and change nappies. Most of the things I see about maternity leave on social media are 'look at me doing all of the things'-type posts about how thin I am or how good at multitasking I am. But I've now tried to follow more of the 'if you have managed to keep the baby and yourself alive for the day, that's all you need to achieve'-type posts. This is the philosophy I have decided to live by. The health visitor suggests getting a sling so if I can't settle the baby, I could pop him in the sling and whip up a meal or do some washing. I stupidly tell her we actually have one and of course she asks me to get it. I do as she says, and she then proceeds to get me in it. I don't feel entirely comfortable but, before I know it, she's trying to slot a screaming Arthur in. I'm confused by what she's doing. And so is Art, evidently. I don't think I have heard him scream like this ever. Just when I think I'm going to explode with embarrassment as she's telling me how much he'll like being in a sling, Rhys bursts in. Seeing the 'make it stop' look on my face, he unwraps me, gets Arthur out, cuddles him and gives the health visitor a glare. Thankfully she uses this as her cue to go.

As soon as she's gone, I Google fore and hind milk. Around 20 per cent of the articles I read say that different kinds of milk are a thing, and the other 80 per cent say it's all bollocks.

I'm lying awake in bed thinking about what the health visitor has said today when I hear Arthur stir. It's 01:00. My mind clears, and I walk over to get him and take him downstairs for a feed. I must have been too eager as, after a couple of seconds, he falls asleep on my nipple. I'm annoyed and frustrated and I shake him awake. And then I realise I'm shaking him a little harder than I intended. He bolts awake and, rather than continuing to suck, he cries. Of course he does. I hate this, I hate every part of this. I wish more than ever that something will happen to this baby to make him go away.

'No!' I say to myself, out loud I think, and I start to cry at what a vile, evil witch I've become. I tell myself that I don't deserve to be alive and to have this baby when I can have such awful thoughts about him and now, evidently, do such horrible, unmotherly things to him. I try to cling on to the fact that I'm a ball of hormones still and every new mum must have these thoughts. They don't make me evil; they just make me part of the new mum club and just like any other woman whose body is a rush of hormones and whose thoughts are unaccountable. I'm trying to excuse myself. I'm shocked at what I've done but not enough to mention it to anyone.

11TH JULY

Out of the blue, I get a text from a friend of Bec's sister, introducing herself as working for Bluebell, a charity in Bristol which specialises in helping women and families experiencing postnatal mental-health problems. The text says I can call her any time so I just press call. A lady called Paula answers as I slowly retreat to a chair in the kitchen. A hard, wooden, dining chair I find I am sitting on a lot. My Safe Chair.

Arthur is sleeping so I just start rabbiting away to her. Talking to her, I feel safe and don't want the call to end. The difference with Paula is that she's been there, she's had this, and she seems to know EXACTLY how I feel. This is the first time I've spoken to anyone who gets it. Everyone who has been to see me and assure me that I will get better has never been there. They are convinced I will get better but none of them has actually felt what it feels like to be so utterly, totally useless.

She tells me she wishes there is more she could do for me, but she only covers Bristol. She reassuringly tells me to call any time and that if she misses my call, she will find time to get back to me, and I know she will never break that promise. Arthur starts to stir so I panic, thank her for her time and hang up.

The Crisis Team comes again. I tell them about Paula and ask if there is something similar to Bluebell in Cheltenham. They tell me about Pandas, a foundation that gives support and advice to parents about perinatal mental illness. Brilliant! But the Cheltenham branch shut down last year. Oh.

13TH JULY

A different lady is here from the Crisis Team. She's brought a trainee colleague too and they have come to check how I am. I take them into the lounge and they both squash onto the small sofa while I make myself as small as possible on the big sofa. I moan at them, they do sympathy head and face at me, nodding along and agreeing how rubbish I must feel to have had such little sleep. I realise I'm not here to entertain them so I stop – I have nothing else I want to share and I can't be bothered to talk any more. The first lady then takes her opportunity to tell me a good way for reducing anxiety. If I'm feeling anxious and I'm hot, I should move to a cool room or take a cool shower. If I'm feeling anxious and it's dark, I should move to a light place. Every ounce of my being knows I am never going to put this into practice. I am anxious all of the time, it doesn't matter if it's hot or cold or light or dark, so I'd be constantly moving or getting wet. I find getting in the shower is daunting as it is. I'm not sure why. It should be nice to feel clean, especially with the night sweats and leaky boobs. But I just don't want to step under the water. Maybe it's something about being naked and vulnerable. I just can't fathom it, but I know I avoid it as much as possible. The idea of anyone going to stand under a cool shower when they REGISTER they are anxious AND in a hot place, is mind blowing to me.

As they leave, they tell me the Perinatal Team will come to visit me on Monday. I close the door, give Alma a hug and look longingly into her black eyes while holding her soft ears. 'What am I going to do?' I ask her. I silently know she wants this all to be over too.

14TH JULY

I'm sitting in a shitty little tumble-down shed on the boundary line and it's freezing cold. Not only do I not want to be here, I'm still trying to process why I came and why I let them talk me into things I so clearly don't want to do.

It's cricket match day, and it's horrific from beginning to end.

Rhys left early this morning for practice as why wouldn't he? The excitement of a day away from hell couldn't come soon enough. He had programmed the place where they were playing into the sat nav in the mum wagon and all I had to do was to DRIVE to the vet for a check-up for Alma and then DRIVE to the match. I don't know why we haven't put Alison on our insurance, probably because I can't even remember who I'm insured with and it would be me that would have to make the call. And I haven't. And now it's too late. I will have to do the driving.

I didn't know how I was going to do it, but I had to. Rhys had to play cricket as he needed some time away from work and dad to be Rhys. I didn't entirely agree with this, but he seems dead-set on continuing to play the season and his mum says it's a good thing for him. Mums are always right so that's the way it was. Alison wanted to go and watch, which was fair enough, and I wanted to be a supportive girlfriend. The fact that I was scared of the car was just a minor thing in their heads and they are going with tough love. They had had enough. I had done more than the recommended six weeks of not driving after my caesarean, so that was no longer an excuse. I simply had to get on with it.

The drive to the vet was terrifying. I could barely remember which order the pedals were in. A number of times I slammed on the brake, thinking it was the clutch. I'd glance in the wing mirrors, think people were too close and jerk the steering wheel, covering myself in a cold sweat. I swear for part of the dual carriageway I had my eyes closed, just hoping we'd get there or end up in a ditch. Goodness knows why Alison was happy to get in a car with me. Alma and Arthur didn't have a choice.

By some minor miracle, we arrived. I knew I was shaking, so got out quickly and got Alma out of the back, leaving Alison to stay with Arthur. As I stepped through the door with Alma, it suddenly dawned on me how much I had neglected her. I started sobbing silently into her ears, waiting to be called through.

When I had known she had to go in for the second operation, I had started to hope that she would never wake up. If we didn't have a dog, that would solve my worries about the house being overridden with hair and I could finally then cross something off my worry list. Now it was just me, her and the vet, reality dawned and I finally realised how very close we were to losing her. I'm devastated with myself, I'm hollow, I'm heartless. Alma is my absolute constant, never judging, never answering back, always wagging and very huggable. I absolutely, never ever want her to know in her doggie brain the horrid thoughts I have had.

I bent down and bundled Alma up. Thank goodness she was still here with us. On examination, the vet recommended it would be best if she wore the cone for another week as the wound had not totally healed. Oh, that's not great news – we were supposed to be taking her to the cricket and her cone was at home.

As we got back in the car, I told Alison that Alma needed her cone back on and I had left it at home. Dilemma – did we take her to cricket without her cone, go back and get it and take her, or go back, put her cone on and then go to cricket without her? My decision-making ability was at zero. I looked up the destination of cricket in the sat nav and looked at the screen in horror when I saw that it was an hour and six minutes away. Thinking Rhys must have made a mistake when he was programming it, I called him.

I couldn't believe it was right – why on earth would he think it was okay for me to drive so far to somewhere I had never been before when I'd hardly driven in the last few months? This really was tough love. I drove home and was very, very close to saying we wouldn't go but I had to. I stayed in the car with Art, lip trembling, deep breathing, while Alison took Alma inside, popped her cone on, gave her a treat and told her to be a good girl.

When we got onto the motorway, I was relieved. I told myself I just had to keep going, in the left lane, and keep rabbiting away to Alison to take my mind off how mad I was with Rhys and her for thinking this was okay. Ninety per cent of my mind was preoccupied with swerving into the ditch at the side of the road. I thought about how it would feel to be in a car accident. What if I survived and Alison didn't? What if we all went, what would become of Rhys?

Rhys was pleased to see us turn up. He went to borrow an umbrella from one of the boys to get Arthur out of the car as, from out of nowhere, the black clouds had started to assemble and it was chucking it down. I was in thin fisherman pants, a T-shirt and no coat.

I couldn't say anything, I just stared at him, shaking, hoping he'd thank me or congratulate me or something.

'You'd better not ruin this for me', he said and took Arthur to meet everyone.

I stood there in shock, not really knowing how to process what had just happened over the previous couple of hours. I'm pretty sure my mouth was open; I was staring at the ground in the rain. Livid. I was livid. I wanted the ground to swallow me, to be taken off this earth. How dare he say that to me? I want to die, and you have just trusted me to bring your mum and your son out to the middle of nowhere in a killing machine. What were YOU thinking? Did I get back in the car and leave? Did I go and hide? All of me wanted to walk off into the woods and just stay there. It would get dark, I would get cold and hopefully I'd just rot away while they enjoyed their cricket.

Did he think I was making up being terrified of the car? Did he think I was going to have a tantrum in front of his team?

As I was formulating my next steps, I saw him come towards me. I looked up, he put his arms around me and said he was sorry, he didn't mean to say that. 'Want to come and meet the team?' he said, trying to put it behind us. *Like a hole in the head.*

Alison has managed to find a shed on the boundary line. It has a few chairs and cricket bits in, so we set up camp with Arthur, sheltering from the rain. The bench is just at the wrong height to be able to see out, so we have to sit and just look at the inside of the shed or stand and try to make out which one is Rhys. I sit on that bench, staring at the wood, looking at the patterns it makes and wish as hard as I can that this wasn't my life. Rhys comes in to get Arthur and take him to show him off to the team. I'm not sure they're that bothered about having a baby at the match, but Rhys looks so proud.

After about two hours and seeing Rhys get run out, I'm beyond freezing and thank god Alison is too, so we agree it's time to go home. Rhys says he'll wait to see if the rain stops before deciding what to do about coming home, of course he will. He helps us load the car up and waves us off.

All I can think about on the drive home is driving into the central reservation or into the oncoming traffic. I'm so tired, maybe it will just happen anyway. I hope so as, apparently, I haven't the guts to drive into something solid. As long as I'm not around any more, I pretty much don't care. But then Rhys flashes into my head and I know this will make him the bloke whose girlfriend killed herself. And Arthur will be the boy whose mum killed herself. And there's Alison, she would be left picking up the pieces.

Now I'm in bed, Alison and Arthur are downstairs waiting for Rhys to return. I'm annoyed, I could be dead now but here I am, sat in bed again waiting for the day to turn to night and then night to turn to day again and I will continue in this holding pattern until I get some guts to go through with it.

I'm never getting in the car again.

15TH JULY

A few people have mentioned to me that I could try writing down things I have achieved in the day or things I'm pleased about or thankful for. Like a kind of happy log that I can look at when I'm feeling rubbish. I'm not totally on board with this. I know I'm lucky to have a lovely house and fiancé and I've been lucky enough to conceive and have a beautiful healthy, happy baby. But I don't care.

I feel at best drained and just plain blue, and at worse like I want to be sick I'm so anxious and sleep deprived. I have no appetite and I don't care if I live or die but I would prefer to die. But I figure I have to do something to show people I'm taking their advice and not just nodding and smiling, so I take a piece of paper and start writing. I list the amazing fiancé, the lovely house that said amazing fiancé built, the supportive friends and family. I write that I have fed Arthur and I've changed his nappy – woohoo, go me. I feel nothing. I read what I have written and, convinced I can't write anything more for today, I write tomorrow's date and pop the list on the side. I tell myself that I will go back to it tomorrow – I'm sure I'll not have that much to add but I can at least write the same list again.

Rhys comes home from work and notices the note. He asks me what it is and I tell him with all the enthusiasm I can manage, like it's a great thing I'm really behind. He smiles and takes a pen. I ask him not to write anything, it's mine and it's for me. I berate myself for leaving it on the side with the post, idiot. He ignores me and starts to write.

I plead with him not to. He continues. His mum is at the table and stays quiet.

In large letters, he writes 'a fucking amazing fiancé'. I'm furious. That was the one thing I was doing, the one thing that was mine that, even though I thought it was bollocks, I was doing. I helpfully pointed out that I had written 'an amazing fiancé' right at the top of the list. I was in a rage and shouted at him for ruining my list. And there was no need for the offensive language. He rolled his eyes and walked up the stairs. I am right in this, I know I am. I know I am crazy, but I also know I am right. I look at Alison, she's shaking her head and pretending to read the paper.

'I'm right though, aren't I, he shouldn't have done that?'

'He was trying to be nice, Laura.' What else could she say? He's her son.

Great, now I have a pissed-off Rhys and a pissed-off Alison. I knew they hated me, now what do they think of me? I spend all day waiting for Rhys to come home and somehow make it better yet every night I do something to ruin the time I have been waiting for. I feel like I should be a line in an Alanis Morissette song.

I hate them both right now. They have been against me wanting to get Arthur into a routine, reading any books that suggest that, so I have just given up. Now they both think I had no right to get annoyed. 'If you want him in a routine, Laura, you're with him all day, you will have to do it' is the response I would get. 'Yes, but I can't put a routine in place and you not be on board otherwise you won't follow it and then what's the point?' 'You tell us what you want to do, and we will do it.' Silenced, I had been silenced. Of course they knew I wasn't going to do anything. I found it hard to even decide what to wear in the morning, let alone research how to get a baby in a routine, decide the method I think will suit us and then go for it. The health visitor wouldn't help – apparently the advice is now to feed on demand, not like when my mum brought us up. I couldn't be arsed, I wanted to die. They know that.

I get a beer from the fridge and go upstairs. I know the only way to move on from this is to apologise. I know I'm not wrong on this. But it's two against one so I must be. I go into our room and Rhys is having a shower. 'I brought you a beer. I'm sorry, I just…' My voice peters out, realising there is no point saying I was sorry and then going on to explain how, ultimately, I am right. Rhys doesn't want to talk to me, but I sit on the bed, frozen to the spot, knowing I have to resolve this so we can have dinner and I can finally get into bed.

He gets out of the shower, gets dressed and lays on the bed. I think and think and think of what to say and I can't think of anything, so I just lay with him. Five minutes must have gone by and I come out with, 'I know this must be hard for you too, I'm sorry.'

'It's okay.'

'Do you think we should speak to someone about *your* mental health?'

'No, I'll be okay.'

'Okay. Can we go downstairs, have a drink and make some dinner with your mum?'

'I'd like to chill here for a bit, please.'

'Okay.'

CHAPTER 4

THE A-TEAM ARRIVES

16TH JULY

Today, as promised, there is a knock on the door and it's three more strangers who tell me that they are mental-health nurses from the Perinatal Team. Every day, more people. I can feel my level of anger rising every time I know I'm going to have to tell them the story from the beginning. I start to feel a real guilt about using all these people's time when, the truth is, I'm just lazy.

I offer them a drink and they all decline. I'm getting the vibe that's what they are told to do but I can't stop offering, I am my mother's daughter. I don't even know what 'perinatal' means, but I like the look of the lady who sees there is no space left on the sofa so she just sits cross-legged on the floor. When I offer her my seat, she does a 'don't be so ridiculous' face. I like her. This lady is called Kim and she starts to explain that perinatal means 'until the baby is one' and that they will be taking over from the Crisis Team from now. Good. They need to do that, the Crisis Team is running out of ideas, I've still not turned lights on when it's dark or had a cold shower when I'm hot.

Kim starts by telling me that I'm not unique and reassures me that this team will help. A swell of tears pricks the backs of my eyes. I don't know what's happened or how she is different from any other nurse who has walked into the house, but I instinctively trust her and everything in me wants to join her on the Alma-hair-and-wound-exploding-remnants-covered rug and hug her and sob on her shoulder. I know I can't do this. But I'm interested in what she has to say, and I think this might be the first time I have engaged with anything in a number of weeks, if not months – I can't remember.

Kim talks through what the team can offer, and I silently note that none of the options involves someone who knows what they are doing when it comes to babies moving into our house and helping me look after Arthur. I feel like we are back to square one and I tell Kim this. Thankfully, she looks at me like I've said something ridiculous and I know I have, but it's good to have confirmation. The thoughts of nannies are now firmly put to bed, thank you, Kim.

We then move on to start talking about drugs. They have discussed with the team pharmacist about me starting on an antidepressant, if I'd like to give that a go. I'm happy to, I'll do anything. Kim says she will arrange the prescription and someone from the team will pick them up and drop them round. Wow. She then moves on to ask if I'm enjoying breastfeeding. No one has asked me this before. No, I hate it. My boobs, which used to be my secret weapon at university, are now being sucked on by this tiny human. They are big and veined and they leak. And I can barely look at them. I have to get them out on demand, it doesn't matter who is in the house or if, God forbid, I'm out, although this pretty much never happens now anyway. It makes me so tired and so needed and I have lost every ounce of what used to be me. So in conclusion, no, I thoroughly hate it. Kim smiles at me and at the other two nurses and I'm getting the vibe that this is a good thing and unlocks the next phase of conversation.

These women are good, they were prepared, and they are coordinated. I feel like project 'sort this family out' has been taken up a notch or three. I listen as they talk with Rhys about the option of bottle-feeding Arthur full time as opposed to just the one bottle at night. This will mean that I can start taking different drugs and get some rest without knowing someone will come in at any minute asking for a boob. There is an uncomfortable, scary cloud in my head that has been there, bubbling away for a while. Bottle-feeding means I will actually have to learn how to bottle-feed, which includes sterilising. It appears to be one in, one out with my brain at the moment, so I'm not sure what is going to have to fall out of the back to allow this new skill to enter my life. But we shelve that as something that's going to happen, we just need to work out how. It's all a fuzzy mass of wires in my mind but they end with

Rhys and Alison being able to feed Arthur in the day as opposed to only before bed, so Arthur is not reliant on me and my milk all day. So, I'll just have to work out a way of untangling those wires.

'Have you ever heard of a Mother and Baby Unit?' Kim questions.

'No', I say, keen to hear what they are.

This is a new thing – this is the thing everyone has been keeping up their sleeve, the 'how' in the 'how are you going to make me better?'

'They are specialist units, usually attached to a hospital, where mothers can go with their babies to recover from mental-health illness. This could be an option for you and Arthur', she explains.

'Okay', I say, immediately thinking that they sound promising. And questioning why I have never heard of it before.

'Is there one in Cheltenham? Or Gloucester?' I ask hopefully.

'The nearest Mother and Baby Unit is in Bristol,' says Kim.

'Oh. Of course. I couldn't remember ever seeing a sign for one here or in Gloucester. Bristol is a bit far for Rhys and Alma', I say, looking at Rhys as he stays silent, hanging on Kim's every word.

'It's about an hour away from here,' she clarifies.

'What actually happens in the unit? Would Rhys be able to visit?' I probe.

'You and Arthur would have your own room. You would be under the care of a psychiatrist. They would assess you and, together with the nurses there, decide what would be the best approach to try to get you back to feeling like you again. They are staffed with specialist nurses and therapists who can work with you and help look after Arthur so you can make sure you get the treatment and the rest you need.'

'Okay, I see', I mumble, thinking they sound like the most amazing facilities, as I'm trying to process what Kim has said. I can't believe I didn't know places like this existed. 'How many rooms are there in Bristol?'

'There are just four beds in Bristol,' she says, with a hopeful smile.

'Four!' I exclaim, 'That's very bijou!'

'Yes, I know it's not many. There are 17 units in the UK, some have more beds than others but Bristol is the smallest with just four beds. Birmingham is the next closest to here and they have nine rooms. There are also some units on the south coast and some up north', Kim explains, enthusiastically.

I've stopped listening. Just when I was starting to formulate a plan in my mind, thinking about my brother and his four-bed house in Bristol, I suddenly realise this isn't an option. Rhys loves Arthur, I simply could not take Arthur that far away. There is no point thinking about this option any more.

And then my mind feels like a flatline, brrrrrrrrr.

I know Kim can see I have switched off, so she wraps the conversation up by saying she knows they have given us a lot of information, so she'll leave us to digest and have a think. She'll get the Citalopram to me to start right away. She lets us know the Crisis Team will be here on Friday and she'll come next week. She'll text me to arrange the exact date and time. I agree and stand up to show them out. They are leaving us with things to think about but, in essence, this day is just the same as the day before and the day before that. Rhys has to go back to work. I retreat back to the Safe Chair in the kitchen to wait for him to come home and, somehow, make things better.

I've been tossing the conversation around in my mind and spend the afternoon on the chair asking Alison questions about stopping breastfeeding and how it felt. She fed her boys until she went back to work, where she continued to express in the office toilets. *Enough, you smashed it too, I'm done with this conversation.* So, we watch Wimbledon until Rhys comes home. We discuss all the pros and cons and all come to the conclusion we will gradually move to full-time bottle-feeding. Half of my mind is panicking about sterilising, mastitis, how I'll make a bottle in the night, and what the plan is to gradually reduce boob and increase bottle without my boobs exploding. Ideally, of course, I want a spreadsheet with the whole process in, a step by step of what to do, but I know I'm not going to get that. I resolve to scour the internet and see if someone has kindly noted down what they did that worked and would send me a little chart. The other half of my brain is incredibly relieved to not be on tap 24/7, however that's going to happen.

I feel no remorse or guilt for stopping breastfeeding. It's been seven weeks and I'm sure that's fine. Arthur will not be a failure; he's had a whole seven weeks of my milk and I've hated every moment of it. Every sip he has had directly from me. Even though I got all the pumps before the birth, I had no desire to use them and the thought of learning another new thing made me so anxious, it wasn't even worth thinking about. All the other girls in my group, without exception, had used them so I knew I was a failure for not even trying. I'm pleased I get to see everything boob-related go and I'm actually quite excited about the prospect of wearing tops that don't allow easy access. I think about going back to bras that actually have some support and I can feel some kind of nice in. I also look at the felt breast pads and think about how good it will be to have some kind of odd pagan-type ritual in the back garden when Arthur is fully bottle-fed. I'll burn the pads and the bras in some kind of caldron while dancing around it with my non-dribbling, pert boobs which will of course have sprung back to under my chin. They were not there before I had Arthur but, hey, a girl can dream. I text Ellie and Becca, telling them the decision, and as their positive replies come back I feel good, confident in the decision, we are all in this together.

And then Rhys mentions that his brother has just announced he's getting married in Australia and it's in

November. Boom, my good mood crashes to the floor, to be replaced with fear and a million questions. If I'm not breastfeeding, how will we have enough milk to feed him the whole flight? We're not allowed to take more than 100ml on the flight. We'll have to see a million people I don't know. I'll have to drink; I'll have to find something to wear. And on and on and on. Rhys looks so hopeful; I want to die. I know we are not going, and he knows we are not going. I know I will always have to live with the fact that Rhys didn't make it to his brother's wedding as I'm a lazy, loser of a mother. I smile but no words come out, so it's just left hanging in the air.

As I go to bed, considering the day's news, I start to think if I have made the right decision with this bottle-feeding plan. Formula will be expensive. Arthur spews at least once a day so is this a massive waste? I don't like breastfeeding but at least it's free and I always had my boobs with me. If the bottles will only remain fresh for a number of hours, how will I keep track of this and how will I ever be able to go out of the house for longer than this? My mind closes this idea off by telling me I won't be able to go out for longer than the milk is fresh, so I'll just not go out. So not only is this hell but now, it's confirmed, my world has officially just shrunk down to be simply the house and the house alone.

20TH JULY

Rhys takes Arthur after his early morning feed and I collapse straight into bed. I wake after about an hour with sore boobs. We have replaced pretty much every feed with bottles now, apart from the night-time ones as I guess it's just convenient. I certainly have not got my head around the fact that we all sleep in the loft, the milk and the machine are in the kitchen and Arthur's room is on the middle floor. It's too much for one person to work out so I just try to push it to the back of my mind.

The last few nights, it's seemed like my body has got the message, we no longer need it to produce milk, thanks. So why is it different this morning? Maybe he's not fed enough in the night? But why then would he have been okay being out for an hour with Rhys? Maybe he had fed him a bottle in the park, and he's taken him to work? Maybe I'm producing more now as he needs another early morning feed. All the possibilities swirl around my head, trying to come up with an answer. I walk into the shower and squeeze my boobs until they're sore. I know this is the wrong thing to do but I don't want the milk inside me. If I get mastitis, I deserve it. When I'm finished, they are so sore, they're throbbing, and I find myself sobbing at my wet useless body.

Later that morning, a nurse from the Crisis Team visits to tell me they are signing me off. I'm relieved. I've been nothing but dismissive and disgusting to them and they do not deserve that. They have such a crucial role to play in society. If someone cries for help to the right person, these heroes without capes will visit your house and stop you doing something that could end your life and send ripples across your family and your community for a lifetime. Wow, that is massive. But after that initial visit, I have found that the only thing that seems to help me is moaning to them about how hard I have things, how confused my head is and how scared of my baby I am.

The team works 24 hours a day, 7 days a week. This work pattern is obviously essential for the work they do but by sheer virtue of this fact, it's rare that you see the same person twice. This means you will always be asked to start from the beginning, and this just fuels the rage. Work Laura can't understand how they don't have a central file on me that everyone who turns up at my door has read so they don't have to ask all the same questions. Maybe they do. Maybe they don't have time to read it. I don't know but I want to fiddle with their processes when I'm well and really try to work out how they can continue to be heroes after that initial visit.... One filed for Future Laura.

My care is to be taken over by the Perinatal Team full time. That's good, I like Kim, I think she can help. I just need to listen to her, trust her and do what she says. Kim's got my back, I know it.

21ST JULY

We live in such a friendly street. We bought a 'renovation project', shall we call it, and lived in a small rented flat about five minutes' walk away while Rhys was renovating. We moved in when I was about six months pregnant so we've only actually lived here for a few months now. While we were in the rented place, I'd drive straight to this house after work to see the progress.

I quickly learned that the lady over the road has lived here for most of her life and has grandchildren. She loves children and has been so excited about meeting Arthur. She's invited us to her house for lunch, along with a couple of other girls from the street with their children, who I have got to know since moving into the area. I'm so anxious, I spend most of the morning on the loo. I normally love meeting new people but I'm petrified.

The time comes. I open the door, shove the pram out, down the board across the mud pit before making a run for it through the rain over the street and up her path to the front door. We manage to get the pram in, and I realise that it's going to be in the way. I don't know what to do, I shouldn't have brought it. I just stare at her for a solution, not saying anything, but we are saved by another knock on the door. It's another mum with a slightly older baby girl. She has the same tank of a pram as me and another rain cover we have to find space for. The pram's wheels have left big wet muddy splashes all over the nice clean floor – what a disaster this trip already is. They manage the pram Tetris while I stand awkwardly on the bottom step.

The other mum offers our host some homemade something, and it feels like a stab at my personality. I would normally take things to people's houses when I've been invited but I haven't this time. I haven't even thought of it. While I'm berating myself, there is another knock on the door and it's the third mum. She has brought a platter of crudités, in the rain, that she's prepared herself while she has a baby to look after. I am the worst.

The mums drink Prosecco and I have a glass of water. They know I'm taking tablets and they know I'm struggling but we have not talked about it explicitly and I don't want to.

Once lunch is finished, we go back into the living room and I get a text from Kim. She's going to drop a prescription off. She's spoken to Rhys who has said that he'll pick it up and get it filled after work. I feel like I need to get home so I can see Kim, but I don't want to leave. I go to the front door and text Kim, saying I'm frozen to the spot, I can't move, I don't know where to be. Do I keep trying to persevere and stay here and hopefully the good time everyone else is having will consume me? Or do I go back to my empty, lonely house in the hope that I might see Kim's reassuring face for 30 seconds? She replies as she always does with a suggestion and reassuring words. I go back into the living room and tell the guys I'm going back home. They look disappointed; I have no idea why, why anyone would want to hang out with Miss Miserable is beyond me. The rain has stopped, and I get back across the road with no dramas. I leave Arthur in his pram and go and sit in the chair in the living room window with Alma. Her watching out for her master to return, me waiting to capture a glimpse of reassurance in Kim through the mud-splattered windows.

22ND JULY

One of the mums from the lunch yesterday has texted. She knows I'm struggling, very obviously after yesterday, and has a pal who is also struggling and wondered if we'd like to meet. She was going for coffee with her in a few hours and I could join. It was just going to be in the park and she would be there the whole time.

She'd seen me in a total state yesterday so what's the harm? I might come out of it with someone who talks my language, who understands. I say I'll go.

It was awful. She was totally different from me. She cuddled her little boy and told him how much she loved him; she was happy to breastfeed in a park. She had joined Weight Watchers and was managing exercise; she went into the café to get herself a coffee and piece of cake. She did all of these things and I couldn't do any of them. I didn't love my boy and I didn't have the strength to pretend in front of others. I didn't care about weight or food, and the thought of joining a class or actually doing any exercise that involved me having to put something on other than the four or five items of clothing I was cycling was beyond me. I was just rooted to the chair drinking whatever had been brought to me.

I'd been looked after from the moment I had left the house to the moment I got back. She'd suggested a table, she had bought me a coffee, I couldn't even think about eating. I couldn't do anything, and the other PND girl I was hoping to bond with seemingly did everything so easily and without thought, it just seemed to come naturally. Watching her made my tummy flip and if I could have run, I would have done. If she was suffering with PND, what on earth was wrong with me? Maybe she was over the worst or maybe she was just pretending. Maybe that was the first time she'd been in a café, maybe she made it up about Weight Watchers and exercise, or maybe she was just saying it to a group of mums as she wanted to 'feel normal, fit in', say what she thought she 'should' be doing. I had to think that, otherwise what on earth did this mean for me? She didn't make me feel not alone, she made me realise that not only was I struggling but I was too lazy to even do anything about it.

As we walked away from that coffee, my friend apologised to me. She could see it too. She'd set something up she thought would help, but even she could see it hadn't. She's so genuinely caring, she didn't need to apologise. If anything, I was pleased to have been out of the house for thirty minutes, away from my head and my dark, dark thoughts.

26TH JULY

In the midst of the people coming and going, I realise that my six-week check (which is actually an eight-week check at our surgery, allowing for the logistics to combine a doctor's appointment with an inoculation appointment) is today. Rhys manages to get the time away from work and picks us up with seconds to spare before the scheduled start. I'm obviously anxious that we'll miss the appointment. I've heard from one of my antenatal pals that her appointment was reduced to six minutes as the doctor was running behind and she just got a 'and you're okay, right?' before she had to leave.

The doctor starts by assessing Arthur and ticking a lot of boxes on a form related to his development. It then comes to asking about me. I'm guessing she can see stuff on her screen about my previous visit. I don't know if she feels as deeply awkward as I do but she just tells me to keep working with the Perinatal Team without making any eye contact. In stark contrast to my last visit, I feel this one is more matter of fact and, I guess, less sympathetic. I don't know if I deserve sympathy particularly, but I immediately feel stupid for being in the category of people who can't cope/ be arsed to look after their babies and that information is now available to all in that surgery to see.

27TH JULY

I'm really looking forward to seeing Kim. I hope she has something new to tell me. Something that will give me hope.

Just before she is due to come, Arthur has a bottle, so Alison offers to take him out for a walk. I'm pleased she gets it; it means I don't have to sit in the living room with the door shut trying not to hear every noise he makes. My ears seem to be super-tuned-in to every little peep.

When Kim arrives, Alma is pleased to see her, too. She's finally free of her cone of shame so it's easier to pat her and she doesn't do as much damage to your shins.

I tell her that we are doing well with the bottles and, apart from that one morning, my boobs seem to have totally deflated. I just need to conquer the night-time bottles and he will be exclusively bottle-fed. She suggests that I can continue to breastfeed him at night if that's easiest and I don't know why but I want it to be all one or all the other. I want it to be binary, yes or no, black or white. I tell her about the bottle-making kit being downstairs and us being in the loft, blah, blah, and she suggests getting some pre-mixed bottles and keeping them in Arthur's room. Of course, she is an actual genius.

We then move on to talk about the cricket match. She can't believe I have been. She can't believe Rhys even suggested it, with it being so far away, and I'm pleased that I'm not going mad, HA! She asks when the next one is and it's tomorrow.

She says, 'Just don't go.'

'How can I not go; I have to go.'

'Why?'

'Well, because Rhys wants me to and I want to be supportive and his mum wants to go, and she doesn't have a car here and she's not insured on mine.'

'Well, Rhys can take his mum and she'll just have to sit through the warm up.'

'But then she'll have to be there from ten in the morning until ten at night when Rhys normally gets home from matches.'

'What? He doesn't finish until ten? That's twelve hours!'

'I know, right, they have beers after to celebrate or, more often than not, commiserate. And where they play always seems to be an hour away so that's two hours of commuting.'

'Well, if she wants to watch, I'm sure she'll be fine with that. But you don't have to go.' She pauses. 'Do you actually want to go?'

'Erm, well, no. It's so far away. I hate driving and I just don't want Arthur to puke or me to have to change his nappy when we're out or anything that will mean people are looking at me and knowing I can't do it.'

'Okay, so (a) you *can* 'do it' as you are doing it every day, looking after Arthur, and (b) tell Rhys you are *not going*. You have supported him once but this time, you don't feel you can. Do you have something else you could do that day?'

'Erm, well, my friend has just had a baby and a few of the girls are going over to meet her. The only thing is, she's a drive away and I don't want to drive any more. When I'm in the car, I mainly think about how I can die in it.'

'I'm going to mention to Rhys you're not to drive any more. You're tired and you're unwell and it's got to the point where it's not safe.'

'I don't know if I would actually go through with it. Thank you. I'm sorry', I say while looking at my feet. I don't know if I'm sorrier that I can't go through with it or that I'm making her have to talk to my boyfriend when I should be able to do that.

'I'm sure one of your friends can take you and Art, and if Alison doesn't go to the cricket, she can have Art for a short time while you go. He's bottle-feeding now so you won't feel the pressure to get back.'

'Erm, okay then, I guess I'll just tell Rhys I'm not going, simple as that.' Apparently.

I actually love her a little bit. She's pragmatic, talks straight and comes back with answers rather than more problems. She reminds me of me when I was me.

We talk about how I feel, if I'm enjoying anything. I'm not. I still don't want to be here. I still think the right idea is for me to die or for Arthur or die or for someone who actually can love him to have him. I just can't do it; I've run my course, and this is just too hard. I need it to end.

She says all the right things but nothing that makes me think it's going to come to an end any time soon. She tells me she's going to request an appointment with the team's psychiatrist so we can discuss my care plan. Hopefully that will give us some answers. And if not, I know what I have to do.

28TH JULY

I'm lying awake waiting for any movement from Rhys. Anything to give me a clue he's awake and then I can talk at him and stop listening to all the swirling in my head. I can't get in the car; I have to tell him I'm not coming to cricket. I can feel my heart beating in my neck and I'm really hot. I think about going downstairs and getting into Alison's bed and just hugging her. I think about it but I can't do it. I can't, someone has to make this end really,

really quickly. I put an arm around Rhys. He doesn't wake up but he turns over so I can lie on his chest.

We must be there for about thirty minutes. Him getting some sleep, me just working myself up into a frenzy. All my muscles are tense. As Arthur stirs, everything in me goes cold and I squeeze all my muscles even tighter. *I can't do it. I can't do it. I can't do it. This is hell. This is hell. This is hell.*

I feel like I'm wired.

I need to get up.

I have to get up.

I can't get up.

After another few minutes, Arthur starts crying and Rhys asks me if I'm going to get up and feed him.

I can't, I just can't. I grab onto him harder and harder. I'm crying and I think I'm speaking out loud now. 'I can't do it.' 'I can't do it, don't make me do it, I can't do it.' He jumps up and pulls me off him. 'You have to do it, Laura, he's the most important thing to us, we have to look after him,' he shouts while gesticulating.

I just stare at him, in shock. 'You have to stop relying on other people,' he says, 'you have to pull yourself together, you have to stop relying on your friends and mum to do things for you. People have always done things for you and you just need to grow some and get up and look after this baby.' And with that, he picks up Arthur and storms out.

I don't know what to do. I pull the covers over my head and cry, and cry, and cry. I decide I'm going to stay here all day. If someone comes in, I'll not get out. Hopefully the bed will swallow me right up. I just need some time; I just need some space. I know I need to get myself together, but I don't know how, I just don't seem to be able to. Or maybe it's not that, maybe it's just that I don't want to. I don't want this life; I can't do it any more. I have had virtually no sleep and I can't continue to be on alert all day and all night, buzzing, twitching, worried about things that matter and things that don't, constantly scrolling through the list in my head, worrying about what to worry about next. I can't get out of the house; I want to but there is something inside me that just won't let me go. I don't want to speak to anyone unless it's Kim or Paula, I don't want to see anyone, I don't want anyone to see me and to see me failing, falling apart, breaking up.

I sob, and I sob, and I sob.

I then start to scream.

I don't know how to get the energy out, so I scream. I scream as hard as I can into the pillow. I want to hold it onto my face, but I can't. I'm so useless, I just can't. I think of Ellie and I think of Becca and I sob for them, I sob for what I still want to do to myself, but I can't do it, I'm a failure. Rhys is right, I'm lazy. I have always had other people do stuff for me. At school, at university, at work. And now I have well and truly come unstuck. No one can do this for me, so this is where I have to end.

I don't know how long this goes on for, it could be minutes, it could be hours.

Rhys comes back and sits on the edge of the bed.

He tries to pull the covers off, but I pull them tighter around me and try to make myself as small as I can.

'Laura!' I uncover my face. He looks at me and talks softly to me. I just have to keep going. I just have to keep looking after Arthur. I tell him I know but I can't. I don't want to any more. I'm not sure he knows what to say and I can see his eyes are red and there are tears in them.

'I just want my Beanie back.'

As I start to cry again, I squeak, 'I know, I do too.'

We hug and we cry, and I agree to get up, but I tell him I can't come to the cricket today. He doesn't say anything. How can he?

29TH JULY

Today is D-day. I know they have been planning it for about a week now. I assume trying to keep it secret from me. I'm not stupid, I know Rhys' dad is arriving in two days and there was no chance Alison would stick around to hang out with her ex-husband.

She's been helping me less and less and it's been driving me mad. She's just going about her day, sorting herself out, doing washing, trying to pretend she's not there. It's really winding me up. Either be here and help me or don't be here. That's my black and white thought. By not cooking dinner or not making me some lunch when you make yours is not helping, it's frustrating. I know she's trying to condition me for when she's gone so I ask her outright. It's confirmed that's what's happening. I wish I had the balls to say it's really making me angry, but I don't. I tell myself I'm going to use this anger to pull myself together and prove her wrong. Every part of me knows this is not going to happen but I tell myself that.

I text Mum, saying that I want to get on the train on my own to her house and never leave. I lie in bed thinking really clearly about my bedroom at her house. I think about watching the TV in their lounge with the fire on and then climbing the stairs to sleep for hours. I replay that over and over again in my head until Arthur wakes up and I have to get up. Mum replies but I don't read it, I want to pretend the reply says to go and get on that train and she'll meet me at the other end. As I go downstairs, I can see Alison folding clothes into her case. She's stripped the bed and put the sheets into the wash. I'll need to remake that bed in a couple of hours for Rhys's dad, Richard, and partner, Louise, who are arriving in a couple of days' time. I go downstairs to find Rhys with Arthur. As soon as Rhys sees me, he says he has to go and see a client quickly and off he disappears. I have never known him to 'quickly pop' anywhere so I expect that will be that last I see of him for the day.

I retreat to my chair and let Arthur fall asleep on me. As I reply to my antenatal group, a text pops up from Dad saying he's been to see some friends the night before and both their daughters had PND. I need to hang in there. I assume therefore that they are now functioning human beings who believe there is something to live for.

Rhys bounds through the door a couple of hours later. I think I have moved from my chair once in that whole time. He announces that we should go for Sunday lunch as this is Alison's last day in the UK. I don't move but I start to panic, going outside is my nemesis. It's raining too, what footwear should I wear in the rain?

Has Rhys booked anywhere? Will we walk or drive? I hear him call a local pub; it appears they have space as I hear him tell the bloke we'll be there in about ten minutes. WHAT? The pub is at least a twenty-minute walk away and we have a baby who cannot get himself ready to leave the house, well, not that I'm aware of anyway. He has no clue. I can't believe he's said ten minutes, what a stupid thing to say. When we eventually get there and it's actually been more like thirty minutes, they'll have given our table away and then we'll be in the rain and hungry and what a treat for Alison on her last day in the UK. A great way to cement her never coming back. As Alison and Rhys herd everything into the car, I stand on the doorstep getting in the way. My next-door neighbour walks by and asks me if I'm okay. I can't form words, I'm standing on my front doorstep, activity going on all around and I can't get any words to come out of my mouth. She moves towards me and asks if she can help with the pram. I just stare at her in fear. Rhys appears and says we are fine, thank you.

When we get home from the pub, Rhys quietly takes Alison's bag from upstairs and pops it in the boot of the car where the push chair used to be. I have that feeling of being anxious to catch a flight. But this isn't anxious excitement, I don't think. Maybe there is a tiny part of me that wants the challenge of finally being able to do things on my own. When I was about 32 weeks pregnant, I remember thinking that I had done all the things (pregnancy yoga, buying baby stuff, allocating a room as 'the nursery') and read all the things and I was ready for the challenge of having the baby. I wanted to see what it actually felt like and I wanted to know what my body could actually do. Maybe this is that feeling again, I'm ready to see what I can do.

It's time to go, Alison comes into the kitchen to say bye. I can't get off my Safe Chair. We hug, and cry. As she walks to the kitchen door, I'm rooted to the spot and she whispers, 'You've got this, Canty'. And she's gone. And I'd give anything to be in her position, flying out of this hell to the sunshine. It's winter in Australia but that's detail, she will be a long way away from this.

The girls arrive and they have brought everyone, and they tell me they are going to clean my house. They know the dirt and the dog hair are stressing me out, so they are going to make that better for me. It will just be for a short time, but they figure it will help and they want to do anything they can to help. I'm overcome with everything, I don't know if I'm embarrassed, grateful, hopeless, happy. It's nice to see their faces and I hug them one by one, making all of their shoulders damp.

We all go up to my room and they work like ants as I stare at them in disbelief from my bed. I'm like a dictator telling them which bits wind me up the most and they just make it right. One by one, they just keep going. What a totally, useless, lazy individual I have become. I now have my friends cleaning my bedroom for me.

The text comes from Rhys. His mum is dispatched, he's having a Burger King and then he'll drive back. I go to bed, but I know I won't sleep, least of all because Rhys has driven for a couple of hours, has stopped for minimal time and now he's driving for two hours again. I know he's tired, I imagine he's sad and I imagine he is also scared for how we'll cope without his mum.

30TH JULY

Day 1 post-Alison. Bec tells me she has a week's holiday so she's coming around at 08:00. What a great start to her holiday. I've already told her not to, but she's insisted. My head has told me to try to stop seeing and speaking to people as much as I can so they will forget about me. That way, when I do finally slip away, they won't be too sad.

Rhys got up at 06:00 as I was coming up from the last feed and, ever since, I've been lying awake in my usual routine under the covers, watching the pigeons, wishing I was a pigeon…I hear Alma barking so I know Bec must be at the door, but I can't get out. I lie there thinking she'll let herself in, she has a key, I know that. She knocks again and then I hear her voice asking where I am. I shout back.

I can hear her coming up the stairs. She appears at the door, shocked I'm still in bed. She looks into Art's crib and I assume he's still asleep as she looks back over at me. I tell her I can't get out. Why not? Because I can't. My body starts writhing around like it has too much energy and this is how I'm going to use it up. She offers up a nice shower, clean hair and fresh clothes but I don't care about any of that, I just want to be in bed all of the time. She sits on Rhys's side and starts to chat to me. I can't stop writhing. Arthur stirs and she tries to reason with me to get up. I can't. She tries harder. I feel guilty, I know I'm acting like a child, but I can't help it. I don't want to get out of my bed so I'm not going to.

Bec comes back around to my side, moves the covers off me and starts to pull me out. I'm scared, I'm really scared, I start whimpering but now I'm up. She turns the shower on and guides me towards it. She leaves me to it and I slowly walk underneath the water. I feel like it's nibbling away at me. Every droplet of water hurts and I'm sure it's taking little pieces of skin with it down the plug hole. Bec is like a cheerleader from the bedroom, urging me to wash my hair and condition it and to wash my face and my body. There is so much to do. I turn the water off, I can't take any more, and I appear in the bedroom with my towel pulled tight around me, shivering. Bec is playing with Arthur on the bed and she has laid out clean everything for me. I love her, I fall to my knees and start crying. I need her and I need Ellie so much.

In the kitchen, I sit on my Safe Chair while Bec makes me breakfast and us coffee. I cannot believe this is how she is starting her holiday.

A letter comes through the door, 'Private & Confidential'. It's confirmation of the appointment with the psychiatrist that Kim mentioned. I text Paula to ask her what will happen and if they'll cart me off to the hospital straight after it. I think that's what I actually want. Something has to change, I can't come back from that appointment, straight into this hell. She of course texts back saying that's unlikely, but I could perhaps have a little look at the Bristol Mother and Baby Unit online. I'll do that when I'm on my own.

After breakfast, Bec tells me she has to leave to go and do fun stuff with her family and I'm pleased. So she should. I don't get any enjoyment out of doing anything, it seems, so I really don't want her to be here in that sense. The little voice is also still there telling me to try to distance myself from people. As I go to close the door, she asks me if I'll be okay and of course I say I will. She says that Rhys will be home in about an hour to drive me to the psychologist appointment Ellie has set up for me. I am being 100 per cent looked after. They don't want to leave a gap. I can't imagine the meetings Ellie and Bec must have had to orchestrate this. I owe them so much time back in their lives.

I had had a little mental-health blip when I lived in London (entirely work-related stress). During this time, I had a series of counselling sessions and I'd said to Ellie that I was sure it was the combination of drugs and therapy that made me me again. Ellie remembered this and discussed it with Rhys before asking me if I'd like to try this again. It was something that I should give a go so, together, we had called my health-insurance people and arranged to see a lady in an office on the other side of Cheltenham. And today is the day of the appointment.

As soon as it was booked, it was another thing on the worry list, which was not ideal. How will I get there? Who will look after Arthur? Will she be the right counsellor for me? If this is not the right person, we'll have to start the search for a new person and then I'll have to start from the beginning again, telling them all the stuff that makes me cry. But maybe I won't cry when I tell the new person as I've told it about a million times now so maybe I'm numb to it. And if I don't cry, she won't think it's that bad so she'll wonder why I'm there…

I'm invited into the room and take a seat. It's more of a 'work'-type office than a 'therapy'-type office. There is a flip chart next to one seat, so I assume I'm to take the other seat. She starts asking me basic questions about my history but that's not what I'm interested in talking about, so I start on my own agenda. What's happening to me? How long will I have this? Will I get better? I tell her that if I'm going to feel like this for more than the next few days, I can't do it. I simply can't. I dread every second, every step. I have not looked at Arthur in weeks. I just do what I need to do and then put him in the pram and hope he sleeps. I want him to be sleeping so then I don't have to touch him. I sometimes let him sleep on me but that's only so I have an excuse to sit in my Safe Chair in the kitchen. I'm not sure how many hours I have sat in that chair but it's all I want to do. I don't want to see anyone; I don't want to leave my house. I'm not breastfeeding any more so I know I can be apart from Arthur, he could go live with another family. I'm not sure what would become of Rhys and I but I have stopped caring about that, he probably doesn't want to be with me anyway, I'm a monster of a person who wants to kill myself or my baby, I don't care which but I don't even have the bravery to go through with that. Maybe I'm just making it all up in my head and I do just need to get a grip, get a grip, stop being lazy and look after my baby. Hundreds have done it before me, and hundreds will do it after.

And on and on I go, I can't stop. I'm not sure if she can hear what I'm saying as I'm so hysterical, but I keep going regardless. I know she wants to get back to her form, but I don't want to do that, so I just keep talking. I know it's time to leave but I don't want to. I'm here, Arthur is not and this lady is listening. This is the best place I can be, and I want to be here all day. I can now see panic in her face as she stands and tries to usher me to the door. As I reluctantly get to the waiting room, Ellie is there waiting for me. I clutch onto her and don't want to ever let go.

We walk round and round the car park like we walked round and round the park a month ago, me just talking at her. I know she has to get back to work but I don't want to be alone, so I just keep talking. Office staff eventually start coming out and getting into their cars, so I concede defeat and we get into Ellie's car. I apologise, I'm not sure how I have been so selfish to make her miss so much time from work. I have made a mess of the appointment she has set up. Always being glass half full, Ellie's pleased I have been and at least we have worked out it's too early for this kind of intervention. She's so wise, she's so sensible, I want to be her.

As we get home, I tell her I'm sorry again and she of course tells me not to worry about it. We walk into the house and Bec is sat on the sofa with Arthur and they look so perfect. I don't go to him, I don't look at him, I just sit on the other sofa and download to Bec how the session went. I can't sit still, I have to start pacing around the room while they sit there, Arthur peacefully sleeping on Becca's shoulder. A text from Dad snaps me out of it. He's been to see my brother, I tell Bec. They had a baby a month after us and I have barely been in touch with them. The text cryptically says that they are hoping for a better week next week. Boom, that's a reality check for me. Life is going on outside my bubble. My TWIN brother has had a baby and, reading between the lines, they are not having the best time with a newborn either. It is not all about you, Laura, far from it, you selfish thing.

31ST JULY

I called Paula again today. I'd looked up the Bristol Mother and Baby Unit and wanted to ask her more about it. It just feels good to talk to her and the more I do, the more and more I am convinced that a Mother and Baby Unit is the answer for me. She told me that there weren't many in the country and it was a case of waiting for a bed to become free.

To me, it had always been an option, dangling there, waiting for us to take, but this was the first time that I'd heard that even if you did take the monumental decision that's what you wanted to do, you might not even be able to do it. But I have to just block that out.

Kim drops round to let me know that she's on leave tomorrow so it will be her colleague, Jenny, who will accompany me to the psychiatry appointment. I'm weirdly calm about that, I'm just so desperate for the appointment to happen and for me to be taken away from here.

CHAPTER 5

THIS SHIT JUST GOT REAL

1ST AUGUST

The day of the psychiatry appointment has finally come. The appointment after which something will have to happen. I have no idea what, but this is the meeting that will make it all better. Ellie's mum, Jo, arrives and we set off walking in the 35-degree heat. She said she's happy for me to drive but the car still scares me, so I don't have that option. I used to like the sun but now I just feel it burning my skin. I don't want to put sunscreen on as it's sticky and then I'll have to shower before bed and I've already had a shower today, but if I don't put it on, I'll burn and then I'll look like a Brit abroad and it will hurt and it will be another reason I can't sleep. I don't know what to do so I do nothing about it. My go-to. I'm sweating and thirsty and question whether I've actually put deodorant on this morning. Oh well, I'm going to a mental hospital and it's super-hot – I assume everyone will be a bit whiffy. We find the hospital and very quickly it's apparent that, yes, this is a mental hospital. The first two guys I pass give me a dubious stare while they suck so hard on their cigarettes, I almost expect them to suck the whole thing in. I'm not one of these people; I'm not too sure what I am doing here.

We're informed that the psychiatrist is running late so we sit in the sweltering waiting room. It doesn't really bother me waiting because I know that when I walk out of here, I will be fixed.

I'm called through, so I leave Arthur with Jo and everything else is pretty much a blur. I sob from the minute the meeting starts until I slowly waddle out. I tell the story; I can't quite believe what is coming out of my mouth, but I know it is the truth and that's what everyone has said I need to do – my friends, Paula from Bluebell, my mum, Kim. Just tell the truth and that will mean you will get fixed. Again, I don't want the session to end because that will mean going back to my hell of a reality. The last question the doctor asks me is, 'What could we do to make it all better?'

I can't believe they are asking – surely it's obvious? Take Arthur away from me, simple.

'Apart from that, what could we do?' As far as I know, there is no answer. I don't know it, the doctor doesn't know it, this is just going to be it for ever, and that's why I have to find some way of ending it all. I absolutely have to.

I walk home from the appointment completely deflated. I thought it was going to be the answer to my prayers but, as I had suspected, in the back of my mind, no one is going to help me and there is no answer.

When I get home to my Safe Chair, I sit there and wait for Rhys to come home. Arthur sleeps on me for at least two hours and I text Paula to tell her that they mentioned an MBU in the appointment but they don't think I'm at referral stage yet.

When Rhys gets in, he asks me how the appointment has been. I tell him the four 'solutions' that were discussed and why none of them are the right answer:

1. Do nothing – no, absolutely not.
2. Go back to the Crisis Team coming every day – I can't think of anything worse; I'll have to tell every shift everything and I'm not sure I can take any more whacky solutions that involve hot, cold, light, dark…
3. See if the Perinatal Team can up their visits to twice a week – okay, nice that I'll have someone to moan at more times a week, but how is that going to make things better? And they already come once a week and they have other people to see.
4. Refer me to a Mother and Baby Unit (MBU) – the only viable solution that involves a real change, but it also means taking Arthur away from the one person who loves him.

I try to do something rational to help us make the decision about which one of these non-options is our best bet.

I write the four down and underneath write why each one is a good option and why each one isn't. I realise I have just used a rational process to try to make a decision. This confirms to me further that I'm not broken, I'm just lazy. I can do it if I put my mind to it.

The MBU seems to be the solution with the most positives, but the one major negative is that Arthur and I would have to be there and Rhys wouldn't. Then the nurse who had been at the meeting calls to talk it through with Rhys. They talk for about twenty minutes and I see Rhys smile and even laugh, he's a good guy. When he comes off the phone, the first thing he says is that the nurse has said that an MBU certainly isn't the right option right now. And that is that.

All the other options have too many negatives.

So the nirvana of the appointment with the psychiatrist has come and gone and we are where we have always been: me, a shell of a person, functioning just enough to keep my son alive but all the time thinking I want to be dead. And Rhys desperately trying to hold everything together.

I go to bed knowing Rhys' dad, Richard, and his partner, Louise, will be here shortly. Just as I finish brushing my teeth, I hear the door and feel the guilt of not welcoming them. So, I put on a dressing gown and go as far as I need to down the stairs until I can just see them. I ask how their journey was and they totally understand when I say I need to slope off to bed. This is not how it was meant to be.

2ND AUGUST

I don't want to get up. I don't want to see Richard or Louise. When I told Rhys how hard it was for me to get up the day after his mum left, he was pretty cold about it. 'You got up every morning when my mum was here.' I feel like an idiot, so I have to get up now. I don't know how I'm doing it and I'm leaving it until the last minute, but I'm doing it.

Thinking about it, I guess I didn't want to totally fail in front of his mum. I know we have obviously got a lot closer since all this has happened but I didn't want her to see me like that. But with Becca, I could completely give in. She's one of my best friends and if you can't be vulnerable in front of your best friend, well, then, who can you be vulnerable in front of?

I don't know what Rhys has told them and what he hasn't. They are staying in a flat just around the corner from the house. They come round about ten minutes after Rhys has left for work. They are totally cool and totally 'normal' and ask if I want to go for a coffee.

I'm so angry with myself, so angry. Of course, Normal Laura loves coffee and loves going out. How could anyone find it this hard to go for coffee? There is nothing to worry about, nothing at all. And they don't know Malfunctioning Laura and I really don't want them to see, it's pathetic. I find myself saying yes but with a load of conditions. I'll just go and brush my teeth, I'll just have to get the pram, I'll just pack the bag. Actually, no, I don't want to pack the bag, I'm scared of the bag. I'll take the pram and hopefully he'll sleep if he's just been fed. Right, okay, yes please, but after his next feed. They are of course 100 per cent cool about this, and busy themselves outside fixing the last bits of next door's paving that didn't get done once we had finished our building works.

We head to the Bath Road and they know where they are going, they have a favourite place. Phew, no thinking required. Richard asks me what I want and goes in to order while Louise and I find a spot outside in the sun. *This is nice. This is totally nice* is what my head is screaming at me. But the evil part will not take away that nervous feeling in my tummy. I still feel like I'm buzzing and not one single muscle can relax, not one. As Richard comes back and I'm still jigging around, I know I must be making them feel uncomfortable, so I sit and rock the pram with my foot.

See, this is nice – in fact, it's more than nice. You are out with your in-laws, in the sun and nothing bad is happening. My brain is so conflicted. This is everything I wanted from maternity leave so why is my physical body so tight and stressed and anxious? I keep telling myself that there is nothing at home, why do I want to go home? To do nothing. I should want to be here, enjoying this, in the sun. We can make a coffee last for at least thirty minutes and that's thirty minutes closer to the end of the day when I can take the tablet and try to sleep.

I don't know what we chatted about, but I just want to hug them for being so chilled. There is nothing to see here. Nothing at all.

We get home, Richard goes back to work on the paving and Louise goes for a walk up the hill. I find myself just hovering around Richard, half hoping he'll stop the DIY, pleased that more little bits of our house are getting finished, but feeling guilty, he's on holiday.

6ᵀᴴ AUGUST

It's 30 degrees. The health visitor arrives and asks me how I am. I tell her I'm struggling in the heat wearing the only thing that will fit me and feels comfy over my caesarean scar – fleece-lined tracksuit bottoms. She tells me she brought a baby into this world in Bombay when it was hotter than this and coped. She put damp flannels over a fan apparently. That's me told.

I tell her about my PND diagnosis. She nods, seemingly knowingly, and tells me about her daughter. Apparently, she was diagnosed with PND when her baby was just a few weeks old. I ask how she's getting on and she tells me she's finding it worse now the baby is a toddler. Brilliant.

7ᵀᴴ AUGUST

I have to go, I absolutely have to go to the pharmacy to pick up more antidepressants. Richard helps me adjust the straps of the sling so they feel comfortable and then slots Arthur in. His head barely pops out of the top.

I have the prescription in my hand, with my maternity exemption card and my phone and keys in the other hand. I tuck a muslin into the waist strap, and I figure I'm ready to go.

And I'm out. I have no bag, no food and no nappies.

The pharmacy is only about five minutes' walk away. The sun is shining and I can do this. A man holds the door open for me and smiles. This is okay. The shop is empty, so I get to the desk at the far end and give my prescription to the lady behind the counter. She says nothing but gives me a pen to complete the back. Of course, idiot, I could have done that at home. She asks me if I'm coming back or if I'm going to wait. Apparently, the wait could be up to twenty minutes. Panic, I hadn't factored this in. Its 10:00 on a Tuesday, how many prescriptions can they have to fill? I don't have milk for Arthur. What if he wakes up? I quietly mumble that I'm going to wait. She gives a loud sigh at me, turns around to the pharmacist, rolls her eyes at her and says, 'She's going to wait.' I stand there in disbelief. I would normally say something cynical but that Laura left me long ago, so I just walk away from the desk and have a quiet sob to myself. How can anyone be that rude? In front of a customer? When they are filling a prescription for antidepressants AND the customer evidently has a tiny baby strapped to her? Wow, the disbelief turns to anger as I suck my tears back in and wipe my nose on my son's muslin.

After about three minutes, the tablets are ready. She makes me recite my postcode and thrusts them my way. I take them politely, say thank you and resolve to switch pharmacies as soon as I get home.

9TH AUGUST

A private and confidential letter arrives with my name on it. It's a write-up of the meeting with Dr Morgan, the psychiatrist, and it's four pages long. I retreat to my Safe Chair and read it. It shocks me. I can't believe those words came out of my mouth. I really am a mess. I pop the letter back in the envelope and leave it on the bench for Rhys to read when he gets home. But when I think of Rhys, I think of the part where I've said (and now it's captured in black and white) 'our house is the embarrassment of the street'. I knew what I meant when I said it but the letter doesn't have any of the nuance. He'll be devastated when he reads that. His blood, sweat and tears are in this house. I take the letter upstairs and put it on the steadily growing pile of letters for Future Laura to deal with. I go back downstairs to my chair and think about what Rhys actually needs to see in that letter. Hmmm, actually, quite a lot. So I go upstairs and get it and put it back on the bench. I'll let him read it and then I'll explain that I just meant that our front garden is mud and we haven't finished the porch and we have two big planks joining the front doorstep to the pavement. And that I know all these things will get sorted, and I didn't mean any offence, and I love the house. Oh, it's going to kill him.

But he has to read it, he has to see the recommendations.

12TH AUGUST

I realise I have not answered texts or calls from Mum for a while when one pops up on my phone. She's booked a train to come and see us. I should feel happy, I should be excited, but I don't want to see her. I've done so well at pushing her away, I don't want to remind her of me. But she sounds determined, not like my mum at all, she's coming.

Rhys has arranged the trip with her and goes to collect her from the train station. As I meet her at the door, I crumble into her. Totally and utterly – I feel like the batteries are out and I'm ready to give up. I want to disintegrate right there in her arms.

13TH AUGUST

Kim is coming at 11:00 with a couple of colleagues. They want to talk options as we will have had time to digest what the psychiatrist has said. She texts me to ask if Rhys might want to talk to one of the nurses on his own. I ask him and of course he says no. He wants everyone to meet together and discuss me. It's all about me, I'm fed up with it.

I take up residence in the Safe Chair while Mum makes scones. I tell her that they won't accept anything, but she insists she's just making them for the freezer.

The doorbell goes and Mum jumps into action. I hear her introduce herself in her telephone voice. She shows them into the kitchen. Every other time Kim has come, we have sat in the lounge – this must be serious. They are all talking.

My mum talks over Rhys and I can see him getting frustrated. Kim wants to hear from Mum and Rhys what they think is best for me. Mum apologises to Rhys and, with tears in her eyes, says that of all the options, she thinks a Mother and Baby Unit would be the best and offer relief for the family. I feel like I'm in a computer game in a parallel universe. I know what's going on, but I don't have any control over it. My thoughts and actions have been analysed and my future is being decided.

With agreement from Rhys and I, Kim says she will put together a referral for Arthur and I for a Mother and Baby Unit. She has been working with me the closest and I sense this was always going to be the outcome of this meeting. I trust her implicitly.

And then, just like that, they're gone.

I hang onto Rhys, sobbing and repeatedly telling him I am sorry. He pulls me away and looks me full in the face. He wipes the tears from my chin and tells me that there's no need to apologise. The faster he wipes, the more the tears come.

Later, when Rhys gets in from work, he asks me if I want to go for a little walk to discuss it all. I obviously don't know what I want so he bundles Arthur into the pram and pops Alma's lead on and, with the sun melting onto the hills, we wander across to the oh-so-familiar park. When we step through the gates, with us both staring straight ahead, Rhys asks me the question, 'If there were a bed, do you think it's the right answer?' I hear myself saying yes – it's the first positive statement I've made in months and I feel a tiny bit empowered and proud of myself. The actual answer is that I don't really know but I'm pretty sure the right answer isn't no. We walk to the far end of the park, looking like a normal, happy couple with a dog and a baby when little does the world know, we are making a monumental decision about our future, our relationship, our lives.

14TH AUGUST

Kim texts to say she has submitted the referral and there are no beds in Bristol. Crash, that's the end of the 'last hope' option. She suggests I do a virtual tour of the Birmingham unit. I retreat to my chair and Google 'The Barberry'. I click 'play' on the video, my heart in my mouth. The video is introduced by a past patient. She walks through the unit and it's just awful. It looks like a hospital. Little single beds with massive cots and a shared kitchen which looks like student accommodation. I close the browser immediately and tell myself no.

15TH AUGUST

At 06:00, Mum comes through to Arthur's room where I'm feeding him. She talks at me; I haven't got the energy. I tell her I don't want to do anything. Nothing. I could sit on this sofa all day and stare into space and that would be fine. She encourages me to shower while she burps Arthur.

I don't want to. I don't want to feel nice; I don't deserve it. We chat some more. I tell her how 'nothing' I feel. Totally empty, devoid of any emotion other than sadness, dread and anxiety. All of the bad ones. I don't want to move, I don't even want to achieve anything, I just want all of this to end. Right now. She takes Arthur off me and tells me to go and have a shower and to meet her in the kitchen where she'll have made me some breakfast. I don't want to do any of this, but I think I'm close to breaking my mum and she doesn't deserve that, so I do it.

When I appear in the kitchen, she is changed, Arthur is cooing away in his bouncy chair and she has Alma at her feet. She springs into action to make my breakfast. I tell her to chill. She can't, ever.

My phone beeps and I read a text from Jenny. There is a bed in Birmingham. I can go and visit but she needs an answer by this time tomorrow if we're going to take it. I thought beds didn't come up very often and I was only referred a matter of hours ago. I'm suddenly terrified, this thing we have been talking about that might happen in the future is actually happening right now. I look again at the text and I can see that my hand is shaking with shock. Or is this nervous excitement? I call Rhys but there is no answer. A million things go around in my head. This is definitely something I have to do, right? But how can I actually sort myself out to go? What will Rhys do without Arthur? Is this a last resort? What if it doesn't work?

***

Its 12:00 and Rhys comes in through the back door. I'm sat on the chair, holding Arthur. I've been crying most of the morning but seeing him opens the flood gates. I can see the tears dripping from my chin and onto Arthur's downy head. Rhys comes straight over to me, kneels down and asks me what's wrong. I show him the text. He asks my mum to leave and scoops Arthur and I both up. I can feel myself having a panic attack. He just holds me, and I never want him to stop. I don't know how long I'm there. I can see paint on his shorts, and he smells of dust. I ask him to go and find Mum. He doesn't want to leave but I assure him I'll be fine for five minutes. Alma has gone so I assume Mum must have taken her to the park. Rhys is not gone long and returns with both of them. He and Mum have tears in their eyes. Alma is still wagging her tail and her tongue is still hanging out of her head but as she looks at me, her eyebrows go into sad mode and I know she knows something is not right. I hug her from my chair, and she lets me.

I reply to the text to say I'll take the bed, I have to. Everything then seems to go into slow motion. I can give up, very soon I can give up and it will all be okay. I don't know what will happen after I have given up, but I know that very soon I can.

Rhys goes back to work and Mum takes Arthur and me upstairs into our bedroom. She asks me where we keep our cases. I don't know – not only am I a useless mum, I'm also a useless, disorganised adult who doesn't have a spot for the suitcases. I can't even think about it. This is all so very surreal.

Mum is saying and doing sensible things in an effort to pack for an undefined period of time in a mental hospital. I can't find my checked shirt; I look over and over again in my wardrobe. I'm obsessed with finding it. The more Mum says it doesn't matter, the more and more wound up I get. I don't know how she can't realise that it does matter. How could I have lost it? Mum continues to try to have rational, sensible conversations with me about what I might like to take but I just sulk, trying to work out in my mind the last time I might have worn it. Maybe if I sulk long enough, I won't have to go. She makes me try some things on and they all fit. Things I have not worn in years. I'm pretty surprised so I go to the scales and realise that I'm lighter than before I was pregnant. I should be happy about this, right? The battle in every woman's life is for the numbers to be less every time you stand on the scales, right? I see Mum pack my hairdryer – I would never have thought of that and can't imagine I'll need it but I don't say anything. I then start to take charge and look at my toiletries. One of the things that has always stood in the way of me ever having a spontaneous sleepover is that I wouldn't be able to wash my face and brush my teeth. I'm not that person any more but something inside me still wants to make sure I'll have all the toiletries I need. I look at the perfume and decide no. I look at the makeup. I can't even remember what I used to wear and what order it goes on, so I leave it.

Mum cheerily announces that that's me done, so time to move on to Arthur's little bag. A massive lump appears in my throat. I look at him just wriggling around on the bed. What am I doing to him? What am I doing to my whole family?

I don't know whether to take everything of Arthur's so Rhys won't have to look at his stuff in the house, or to leave some bits so he will be reminded of his son. It's all just too difficult, I can't go.

I text the nurse to ask if we can take the milk preparation machine. She doesn't know so she has to call the hospital. I sit down on the Safe Chair to wait for the reply. About an hour later, it comes and it's a no.

Panic. How am I going to make him milk? I don't know any other way. Will someone be able to show me? Better still, will someone make it for me? I reply 'okay' while thinking how little I know about what's to come. This is another reason on the mounting list of reasons why I shouldn't go. But I know I have to do it, milk machine or no milk machine.

I'm evidently too weak to actually go through with it and kill myself, so it seems my sole option is now The Barberry.

CHAPTER 6

ADMISSION TO
THE BARBERRY

16TH AUGUST

As I'm stood in the McDonalds queue, surrounded by the hungover and waiting for the worst cappuccino I've ever tasted, all I can think is, *I'm on my way to a mental hospital... How did this happen...?*

We pulled over because Arthur had started to cry. We hadn't even left Cheltenham. I cry on and off on the journey. During one of the rare non-crying moments, I call my dad to tell him what is happening and have a surprisingly frank conversation about where we are going and how it is the last resort. The truth being that no one really knows what is going to happen.

We pull up to the hospital complex. We dump the car as close as we can and proceed to put what will be my little life for the foreseeable future into the pram and then wander somewhat aimlessly around the campus for about twenty minutes, looking for the place I don't want to find.

And then we find it. 'The Barberry – The National Centre for Mental Health.' Wow, that's impressive – we are about to walk into THE NATIONAL centre for mental health. How on earth have I ended up here?

In hospital, everything starts to go into slow motion. My brain can't process everything and I can't actually form words to tell the receptionist why we are here. I hear Rhys saying something and then a lady appears and introduces herself as Jan. She's come from the Chamomile Suite where my room is, she'll take us there now and introduce us to my named nurse. That's when the hysteria starts and I can't help but wonder why Jan looks surprised – surely everyone coming to the ward is bawling their eyes out, right?

She leads us to Room 7, where there is what appears to be a night-club bouncer sat outside my door, just staring into my room. I'm crying hysterically and now I'm shaking too. Why is he there? What an odd place to choose to sit and why is everyone else just ignoring him? I don't hear anything anyone is saying to me as all I'm focused on doing is sobbing and asking who that bloke is and why is he there. Again and again. Why won't they answer me? Why won't they shut up and just listen to me?

I don't know why, but I had assumed everyone on the ward would be female. Jan is relieved when a couple of nurses turn up and she can leave. The nurses look as shocked as Jan that I can't stop crying. I look around. The view from my window is of a wall, the bed is single and the cot is massive and old skool, nothing like his petite Danish job I have at home. The wardrobe has no door, no rail and a sloping floor. There are no handles, no taps and no hooks. It suddenly dawns on me that the reason is so that you can't hang yourself. Yes, of course, I'm now in a mental hospital where people are suicidal and try to kill themselves. I was suicidal, that's right, I wanted to kill myself. Let's make it hard for them to do that by not putting handles or hooks or rails in the rooms.

I know I absolutely can't stay here.

I know I thought I could, but I just can't. I need to go home and that's where all my focus now is, going home with Rhys and Arthur and all our things. I will try harder when I'm there, I have to. I'm not staying here.

One of the nurses, Carly, is keen to get through her list of paperwork and so she ploughs ahead with Rhys, working together to make a list of everything coming out of my bag. This is a waste of time as far as I'm concerned as everything is going to have to go back in.

As I keep swinging between calm and hysterical, Carly suggests she could show me around and that might make me feel better. There is not much point, but Rhys is encouraging so I follow her. Of course, we have to negotiate Staring Chap who I have now learned will be with me at all times, watching my every move, until I'm deemed to be no threat to myself or Arthur. We turn right down the corridor and, as I look up, I see a lady in dark glasses wearing a long black cardigan coming towards us. Quickly registering she is a patient, I smile and say hello, but she just keeps singing happily to what she is listening to and staring straight ahead. As we go into the sad-looking crèche, there is another patient, hunched on the floor next to a large teddy bean bag, cushioning a tiny baby with a shock of black hair. As we walk past, Carly introduces her so I plaster a smile on my face and say hi. She looks up and says in a monotone voice, 'I've just fed him six ounces and he's puked five', and turns back to look at her baby. Carly brushes it off with a little laugh and on we continue on our merry tour.

The outside space is surrounded by a high barbed-wire fence and the dining room and kitchen look equally as empty and daunting. We make it back to Room 7 in a bit of a blur, where I find Rhys making a little home for everything. He and the nurse are discreetly making a body map of Arthur, looking for any bruises or scratches. I look at his little vulnerable naked body as they scour it for marks, just to be sure he's not injured in any way. I assume they will repeat this to check if I'm doing anything to hurt him in the next few days. What a monster they must think I am.

The hysterical crying turns back on as they proceed to metal-detect me with a wand. I can't help but feel like I am being admitted to a prison. How did it get to this? I don't belong with the crazy singing lady and the goth – seriously, this is not the right place for me. I thought it was but it's not, so the sooner we stop wasting everyone's time the better. These beds are like gold dust, guys; let's keep them for people who need them. Sorry, I'm just lazy and somehow they mixed me up with someone who deserves help. I don't, I just get through life by asking other people to do stuff when things get hard and I can't be bothered to look after a kid. Sorry, oops, pardon me, we'll be leaving now…

Five minutes later, we are in a room with a psychiatrist, Dr B.

He's charming, funny and calm but, despite this, I still let him know that we are going to be going home. He acknowledges this but asks if he can ask a few questions. In about two hours, we go through a brief history of our life, leading up to driving to Birmingham and being here in this hospital with the other crazies. The doctor seems to think I am ill too. How are people not seeing through me?

I start to relax and even laugh in the interview and, as I'd felt on so many occasions, I just wanted to be in this room, chatting to someone who will listen for ever.

Dr B urges me to just stay for the weekend and suggests that we can reassess on Monday. Agreed, I'll stay for the weekend. We will continue with the Citalopram I'm on but he'll also add in some sleeping tablets and some 'just-in-case Prozac', which I can ask for if I'm feeling incredibly anxious. It's important that I start to feel relaxed and get as much sleep as possible, drugged or otherwise.

Rhys walks me back to Room 7. 'I'm proud of you for agreeing to stay, Beanie, I think it's the right thing.' He looks at me. 'Thanks,' I say while looking at my feet on the lino and trying to keep the tears in.

'Remember, life at home is not working. Your whole life is in the kitchen, like a terrified, caged rabbit. You don't want to do the rest of your maternity leave like that, do you?' 'No, of course not, I'm staying,' I say, finally knowing he's right. Being home was the worst, the absolute pits.

There is nothing else to do but for Rhys to say goodbye and for my stay at the mental hospital be a reality. As a nurse walks us all to the back door and I cry saying goodbye, Rhys puts a massive smile on his face and tells me it will be okay and that he'll see me soon. And that's it. My tears are for a dad not being able to see his son and for knowing it is all my fault. How did it get to this?

As I walk back to Room 7, I don't know what to do with myself.

I sit on my bed just listening to the noises of a mental hospital.

And then Staring Chap I have been so scared of asks me if I want to make a cup of tea. I don't really, but I'm so heart-warmed by the fact he's asked me, and he has such a kind voice. 'What will I do with Arthur?' I ask. 'I can hold him.' Errr, okay. I pass him over and walk to the kitchen. When I come back, I see this tiny white milky baby in the massive arms of this once-scary man who is now cooing away at Arthur while he smiles back. I smile too. Not that I feel anything inside, but I know this is nice and, for the first time, I feel like I could be looked after here.

I ask the Staring Chap about his role (he's a Health Care Assistant, they shorten to HCA) and his family and his life, while I stand at my new front door drinking my tea and looking at the pair of them swaying.

About an hour later, Sammy (I found her name out from Staring Chap, she's the dinner lady) pops her head into my room to tell me dinner is ready. Dinner, of course, I had to eat. Friday night, Quorn Kiev night, yummo. I sit alone in the dining room texting Bec and Ellie to tell them a bit about the events of the afternoon and how Friday nights seem to go down on the ward. It is so quiet, just me and the Quorn Kiev.

Back in my room I am reunited with Arthur and Staring Chap. It's time to bath Arthur as it's nearly bedtime. I kind of expect there to be a mass bathing session but everyone seems to do their own thing. I feel silly asking if I can bath my own baby, but I don't know where the bath is or if I'm allowed or if there is a bath session about to happen and it's on a timetable I have not seen yet. I'm relieved when he says of course I can bath Arthur and he goes to get a nurse.

As I stand in the entrance to my room with Arthur, looking down the long corridor for him to come back, I spot a very glamorous nurse walking towards us. She's incredibly patient with me, shows me where the baby baths are stored, and we bath him together in my room. We get him dry and she asks me where his pyjamas are. Well, he doesn't have pj's, he's only ten weeks old. Should he have pyjamas? He changes about four times a day, so I hadn't categorised his babygrows into pyjamas and 'day wear'. God, I'm such a shit mother – 'No, he doesn't have any'.

'Oh well', she says, 'let's put him in this, this is lovely.' Crisis totally averted by the kind, calming words of the nurse but I turn it over and over in my head – what a totally crap mother I am not to even have pyjamas for my child. Why don't I? Why has no one mentioned it before?

As night time comes and the shift changeover takes place, I try endlessly to explain to the nurses that I usually hand Arthur to Rhys at about seven, have my medication and then go to bed. But medication isn't handed out until ten. Ten! I haven't climbed into bed after ten for about six months. Well, that's not going to work. I start to panic as I can see another three hours of being awake in front of me. I need to be asleep/passed out by eight as I'll have to be up in the night.

After a lot of activity, and me endlessly trying to explain to the very lovely, very large-bosomed African lady how to swaddle a baby, it's agreed that I can be drugged early, hand Arthur over to the allotted HCA (there are so many of them) and go to bed. It feels odd putting my pyjamas on with so many strangers milling about outside the room, fully dressed including outdoor shoes. It feels even odder handing my baby over to this lady, an HCA I don't even know the name of, but on the rota she's assigned to Arthur for the next four hours. I don't feel anything as she walks down the corridor smiling fondly at him. I wrap my dressing gown around me and stand at the door, staring down the corridor and waiting for someone to appear with drugs. When they do, it's nearly 20:30 and I'm just on the edge of debating if I should step out of my room and try to be assertive. I down the drugs in front of the nurse and go to snuggle into my single bed with the plastic mattress. I search for my list of worries but realise I don't really have anything to worry about in here. Real life doesn't exist any more. I'm in a bubble, and totally cried out.

I must have slipped into a drugged sleep as the next thing I know there is an alarm ringing. I am wide awake and see that Arthur is back in my room, swaddled up tight like a little fajita and fast asleep. Of course he is; the lady who had taken him off me the night before was obviously humouring me. She must have swaddled a million babies in her time and was a total pro. Looking at her handiwork, I can see that there is no chance Arthur would be able to get his arms out of that, even I would struggle. I hear fast feet coming towards my room, but they don't stop. I lay as still as I can, sweating, my eyes open wide and staring through the little window in my door onto the corridor. I see another two people run past, but no one is stopping to get me. It can't be a fire. The alarm suddenly stops, and I immediately drift back into my drugged sleep.

17TH AUGUST

Arthur's crying wakes me up and the familiar feeling of dread washes over me. I quickly realise I'm not at home when someone appears at my door. They have a bottle for Arthur and offer to feed him. Okay, thanks, I say in a confused daze and off they go with him. I get back into bed and wonder what happened in the night. When I went to bed, Arthur wasn't in the room but when I woke up, he was back in his cot. I wonder if he'd been awake in the night at all. I'm not sure he can have been as I woke up to the alarm, so surely I would have woken up to his screams? And how did he sleep through that alarm?

I fall asleep again and when I next wake it's 08:30 and I'm disgusted with myself for sleeping this long. Arthur isn't in his cot this time so I don't see a reason to get up. I pull the covers over my head and fall asleep again. The bottom sheet is all wrinkled on the plastic sheet but, for the first time in my life, this doesn't bother me – I just want to sleep, and I just keep falling asleep so easily, it's hard not to. Goodness knows what I took last night but it's still working this morning.

A knock on the door wakes me again and a nurse walks in with a little cup. She says they are my tablets, so I say thanks and roll over. She then says I have to take them in front of her, so I apologise (of course, you idiot), take them and roll over again.

The next time I wake it's 10:30 and I can hear lots of chatter on the corridor. I'm disgusted with myself and really confused as to why I'm still allowed to sleep for so long when Arthur has been up for ages. The shower in my ensuite turns itself on, which shocks me. Maybe a nurse in the office has done it remotely to wake me up, or maybe it's a sign. GET UP, CANTY! I scrape myself out of bed, put my dressing gown on and poke my head out of the door. There are lots of people busying, so I bravely step into them. I walk down to the kitchen and no one acknowledges me. In there, I find cereal and bread and a fridge full of all the colours of milk. I open all the cupboards up high to find a mug. When I locate the correct cupboard, they are all patterned or have logos on. Was I supposed to bring a mug? I don't want to be the new girl who takes someone else's mug. I stare at them for too much time and then look around the kitchen several times to locate the paper cups, one of which I had used the night before, but there don't seem to be any left. I decide I'll be okay without tea. I make some cereal and walk into the dining room; it's empty. I eat my bowl of cereal in about thirty seconds and in silence, wondering what on earth I'm supposed to be doing. Any minute now, I'm expecting someone to come and find me and tell me I need to attend some kind of therapy session.

I sit for a bit and wait, but nothing. After I've washed my bowl and spoon, I wander back to my room and Arthur is still not there. This is just weird, what's going on? Why am I here and what am I supposed to be doing? I sit on my bed, just waiting for someone, anyone, to acknowledge me. Eventually, I see a nurse I recognise from the day before going past and I hear myself let out a little 'hello'. She stops, turns and gives me a big smile. I tell her I'm not sure what I'm supposed to be doing and I don't know where Arthur is. She reassuringly tells me I can do anything I want to do, and that Arthur is in the crèche. Okay, so, I'd love to go and have coffee with my pals but that's not going to happen. I actually have nothing to do. I can't clean or cook or do any chores as I'm not in my house and there is someone here to do all those things for me. I start to wander to the crèche and when I open the door, I see Arthur with someone I don't know playing with a wooden frame with some hanging toys on it.

I feel something inside – I'm not sure what it is entirely, but think it's something between despair that someone else can look after my child better than I can and pride that he's just getting on with it.

Good, I think, *perhaps I'm not totally dead inside.* I introduce myself to the lady in the uniform and she tells me what Arthur has been up to and what he's had in terms of milk and wet or dirty nappies. Hmmm, interesting, why do I need to know that? It's all a bit awkward so I ask if I can have a shower and she looks at me confused and says of course I can.

The shower is actually really powerful, and I'm surprised. The only problem is that whoever has built it hasn't considered that the floor needs to slope towards the drain. Surely that's plumber 1-0-1. So, the water slowly starts to leak under the door and into my room. I feel like I'm at the local swimming pool trying to negotiate a wet floor, my wet body, my wet hair and dry clothes. As I'm halfway through dealing with the situation, the panels in the window in my door flip and a lady is looking in. 'Just doing my checks', she shouts. You've just seen me naked, lady, and you don't seem very surprised by that. That's the first time I feel like a patient and note that my room isn't private, and I must dress in the soggy bathroom from now on.

At lunch, a few more people appear. Dark Glasses is talking about her wedding. Apparently, she's planning it for when she's out. The bits she's most excited about are (a) when she'll ride along the beach on a black horse and (b) the bit where her new husband will carry her out of the water in her wedding dress. She seems to have confused her wedding with a James Bond film, but no one has a problem with that. We nod – nice! And back to silence.

I am so bored. I don't think I have ever had nothing to do, nothing at all. Arthur has just had a bottle so I decide to put him in the sling and walk around the ward with him, at least then he'll have a decent burp and hopefully a longer sleep. Sitting still just seems such a waste of time.

I walk from my room, into the garden, around the garden and back to my room. I do this several times and then I start to count things. Every time I get into the garden, I make myself do ten laps of it. It's a pretty small garden so ten laps is enough to make me feel dizzy. When I get to one end of the corridor, I do ten squats and when I get to the other, I do five lunges on each leg. After about thirty minutes, I realise I am one of them. I'm one of the crazies.

I get into bed and send Rhys some photos of Arthur looking cute in a towel his friends sent us from Australia. I don't know if this will break his heart and I should just not send anything or if it will make him smile.

18TH AUGUST

Arthur crying makes me come round from what seems like a very deep sleep. I get up to change his nappy and, in this time, someone has appeared at my door with a bottle of milk ready to take him off me. I happily pass him over, thank the smiling HCA and then hop straight back into bed feeling smug. As I lie there, a number of nurses briefly knock on the door and then come in to give me tablets or to do a routine check and leave. One nurse, however, rather than just saying sorry for disturbing me and carrying on with the checks, pops her head through the door to tell me that maybe I should get up and have some breakfast. Well, really, gosh, I'm not just supposed to be lying here like a sloth, this nurse thinks I should get up. My body runs cold and I realise that she's cottoned on, she knows I'm taking the piss and don't deserve to be here. I pull the covers up over my head and try to sleep some more. I can't, her words just keep echoing around and around. So, I force myself to take those first steps onto the cold lino floor and get in the shower.

I have a bowl of cereal while standing up in the kitchen so I can see through the window into the crèche to try to spot Arthur. I wash my bowl and spoon, walk around to the crèche and slowly push the door open. I'm embarrassed that they have had Arthur for so long while Lady Muck showers and eats. But the same lovely nursery nurse from yesterday is there and tells me not to worry. I learn that all the babies have two hours allocated to crèche each day to replicate what it's like to have someone to help look after the baby for some time when at home. That's a relief. I enjoy talking to this nursery nurse – she makes sense, is easy going and just loves babies and children. I ask her a heap of questions about her life, her work and the ward and she chats to me like a real person and I really like her for this, she's on my team.

I understand from our conversation that nothing really happens on a weekend, the ward just ticks by and it will feel different on Monday. Okay, so I have a plan: sit tight until Monday when things will spring into action. I like a plan.

Rhys should be here soon and I know Ellie and Bec are coming this afternoon so I just have to kill the time until they arrive.

Rhys and I are sitting on my bed when someone appears at my door. 'You have more visitors here to see you', she says. I want to cry. I leave Rhys and Arthur and go to the front door of the ward.

Here they are. I feel everything at once – I'm happy to see familiar faces yet I'm sorry that I have put them in this position, using their Saturday afternoon to come to Birmingham to see their crazy friend in hospital. I'm embarrassed that I couldn't cope and seeing them here has brought that home so starkly. I hug them and a silent tear drops. The nurse tells me they have to sign in. We walk up to my room so I can show them around and they make the obligatory 'this is nice' noises. I then take them to the kitchen to make tea before going out to the courtyard to join Rhys and Arthur.

As soon as we sit down, the tears start coming heavily. I'm sad that they have had to come. I'm sad that it's come to this. I'm frustrated that I don't seem to be doing anything but I'm quite relieved that they had the same expectations as me about the intense therapy sessions and are also a bit surprised how quiet it is on a weekend. I tell them that I have agreed to stay until Monday when I have a meeting with the doctor, and we can review. They are obviously pleased to hear that. They know I like a plan and I like to be busy, so being here is pretty much the anti-me. We don't really say that much, and it feels a bit awkward. I guess we are all still just a bit in shock that it's got to this and now we are all having doubts that it will work.

I continue to sob, it just feels like that's what I need to do right now. I have no intention of trying to stop. I think it's my body's way of saying I have given up. All I can pretty much muster is oscillating between thanking them and apologising to them for having to come. I know it will be tedious for them, but I have to get it out.

We hear a shout that it's time for dinner, so I guess this is their cue to leave. I'm relieved in a way, I want them to be having a nice weekend, not stuck in a mental hospital because I'm lazy. I walk them to the door and give them long hugs. I can't hold in the tears and neither can Bec. She's always been a crier; she even cries when the Red Arrows fly over and other such random events. She doesn't know why either, but we love her for it and, to be fair, she's done very well to hold it together until now.

As they walk out, it seems really symbolic for me. They are going back to real life and I'm staying here. In here, in my computer game, living through this period of time and wishing it wasn't reflecting time passing in the real world. And it doesn't matter how many people tell me that in the grand scheme of things, the few weeks spent in here will be nothing in the whole period of Arthur's life. I don't care. I know I will never get to look at his newborn face lovingly. I will never be able to proudly show off my brand new baby. I will never be able to take away the awful things I said about him to real live, living people. That has all happened and I will never be able to erase it or to get the time back and live it differently. This makes me so deeply sad and regretful that I just stand, frozen in the corridor.

An HCA taps me on the shoulder to ask if she can take Arthur while I eat. I snap out of my self-pity, 'Yes, yes, of course, thank you.'

It's Saturday night and I'm sat in the dining room, alone again apart from the lady who served me through the hatch. It's not Sammy, I liked Sammy. It's a younger girl who is obviously gagging for me to finish so she can go and have a proper night out.

I just can't understand where everyone is. There are nine rooms on this ward and it's not that I expected to meet my new best pals in hospital, but I did think there would be other patients to talk to and pass the time with. And with that thought, a stunning woman wafts into the dining room and says in the tiniest voice 'Room 8' to the server who dishes out her allotted meal from the hatch. I sit there grinning like a Cheshire cat trying to get her attention, craving the company of someone not in a uniform. She turns around, gives me a little smile and walks out. Sigh.

19TH AUGUST

It's Sunday and I realise that I haven't been outside the compound since we walked in on Friday morning. I go to the little nurse's office and ask if there is any chance of having a walk. Everyone kind of looks at each other and the only male nurse says that he'll go with me – excitement! He checks with the others this is okay as I go to find the baby sling in my room.

I feel like I'm exiting the Big Brother house and there is going to be a crowd of people outside; I hope they cheer me. James (the nurse) asks me if he should change into his 'normal' clothes and I'm confused for a second. Are we going on a date? He smiles and says that sometimes patients don't want to be seen with a nurse. Ha ha, brilliant, look at me, I evidently don't give a shit, let's go! It dawns on me that he hasn't met Laura Canty yet, he's met a version of her who isn't going to be the same person who leaves this hospital (hopefully). I need to keep the faith, I want to keep the faith, and I'm going to make the most of my time with James. He seems to be experienced and friendly so I'm going to try my best to find out how I make this stay work while we add to our step count.

James knows the university and hospital campus like the back of his hand, so I feel like a tourist on a guided tour and not like a mental lady with her little baby being taken for a walk out of the mental hospital. I can feel the sun on my makeup-free face, I can hear the Brummie accents and at least I can now place my new home on the map. I think I have feelings of enjoyment and positivity, so I ask James if this place actually works. His response (which I will never forget) is, 'Yes, for 95 per cent of people.' I obviously ask if he thinks I'm in the other five per cent. 'No,' he says. 'Just trust the process, Laura, trust it.'

Back from the walk, I lay down and before I know it, I'm asleep.

Sammy wakes me by announcing it's lunchtime. I think I'd rather sleep but if I don't eat now, I'll end up eating biscuits for lunch. I'm back in my room in 15 minutes and set my alarm so I can sleep some more before Dad and Rhys arrive.

I can't believe I'm greeting Dad at the doors of a mental hospital. He doesn't seem bothered, though, so I show him to my room where he shakes hands with Rhys and sits in the high-backed NHS chair. He's brought the biggest box of Fairy non-bio (requested), a cuddly piglet for Arthur and some of the smallest socks you have ever seen. Arthur's nearly three months old but he's always been small so I'm sure they will fit for a bit at least. We chat for a while and then I suggest we could go for a walk as I did one this morning and it was okay. I go and ask the nurses if that's okay. They ask me how I'm feeling and when I'm planning on being back. I tell them I feel nothing and certainly not like I'm going to try to hurt myself and that we'll be about an hour.

As we all walk down the corridor, Dark Glasses is coming towards us with no sunglasses on. Just as I'm thinking *Oh God, here we go*, I hear her say 'Hmmm, your husband and your toy boy, yes?' It takes me a second to digest and then we all have a chuckle to ourselves. She's brilliant. Rhys has shaved his head, so I assume she thinks he's someone new. I've still not seen her with a baby.

We seem to have got into a bit of a routine at night now. I give Arthur to the night-shift HCA allocated to me and go back to my room to do 15 minutes of Headspace meditation while I'm lying on my bed, hopefully not getting disturbed. By the time I've got ready for bed, it's time for drugs to be administered so I hover at my door waiting for the nurse in charge to unlock the clinic. I then read until the drugs kick in. Arthur appears at some point in the night in his cot or in his pram, which I leave outside the door in case the HCA wants to use it to walk up and down to try to get him to sleep. I don't know what time he appears but he's always there in the morning and there is a note of any feed, puking or nappy changes he's had in the night.

20TH AUGUST

Monday is ward round day, the day that, one by one, the patients meet with their consultant and their ever-growing entourage of students to discuss how the week has been and what the plan for the following week will be. Today is my first ward round. I've spent years preparing for meetings and even though I am in a mental hospital, this one is no different. I find the piece of paper that explains my rights on it and write a few little notes (with bullet points) at the bottom. They are:

- Why am I here?
- How will doing nothing make me feel better?
- Phone charger

(My charger and hairdryer have been taken away to be safety-tested. I don't care about my hairdryer, but I keep having to charge my phone in the office, which is annoying for everyone.)

A nurse comes to get me from my room and takes me into a meeting room down the corridor. She opens the door for me and I'm faced with a sea of people, all wide eyed and all with their heads slightly tilted to the side. Sympathy pose. Someone starts speaking and I focus in on him. It's the same doctor I met on my first day here, Dr B. He apologises about how many people are in the room and asks if I mind. I feel tiny in the little wooden chair at the end of the table. I can feel tears behind my eyes already waiting to fall out. He introduces everyone around the table; I don't catch a single name even though I eyeball every single one. They are all very, very still. He asks how I am. Fatal. I say I'm okay because I am. Everyone remains silent and I fear this is a

Louis Theroux tactic. Keep quiet and she will eventually feel like she has to fill the silence.

I figure I should, so I go on to tell them that I don't ever want to get out of bed. Every time I hear Arthur wake in the morning, I can't put into words the feeling of dread and hatred that flushes through my body. Everything prickles and then I feel like a heavy, heavy lump and I lay perfectly still, sweating until the shame is so terrifyingly bad, it takes every single piece of energy and willpower I have to put one foot on the floor next to my bed. Sometimes the other foot joins it but sometimes the fear is so bad that I quickly pull it back in and try to get to sleep as quickly as I can so that time and life can just happen without me being conscious in it. And however bad one day is, and however much I guarantee myself that I've hit rock bottom, the next day is even worse than that. Because I know there is nothing worse than rock bottom, I now know that I have hit rock bottom and the cycle repeats.

I can barely get the last few words out.

The tissue I have is sodden and everyone is staring so intently at me that I feel like they are boring holes into my skin. You could hear a pin drop in this room, and I worry that I have upset the students who are just here as part of getting their qualification – they don't want to be mentally scarred from a regular Monday meeting.

Dr B nods, takes a breath and says some words. I don't hear the words, but I know that I trust him implicitly. Whatever he says, I will do, he has all my faith and more.

He tells me that I need to rest and lean on the staff to help me look after Arthur while the new drugs he prescribed me on Friday have a chance to kick in.

If depression doesn't suck enough, all of the medication takes six to eight weeks to be effective so it's just a waiting game. I've been on Citalopram for what seems like ages and I don't feel any different at all. I ask him why I don't seem to be doing anything and his reply makes total sense. It's hard to treat anyone for a mental illness when they are so sleep deprived. Sleep debt is a thing and, as I have spent weeks getting zero to three hours of sleep a night, my body is massively in sleep debt. A normal symptom of depression is not being able to sleep, so pretty much everyone who comes in I guess is a zombie.

Once I am less of a zombie, they will then start to look at other therapies. Right, I agree to give it another week as an inpatient. I squeak, 'Thank you' to everyone in the room and walk out with the nurse. She looks at me and says, 'Tough, eh?'. I just fold into her and have another cry.

There is nothing like a hug from a plump nurse. She smells of freshly laundered uniform and she hugs with just the right amount of pressure that says, 'Come on, love, you will get there.' Not too lightly so it seems like a token 'I don't want to be here' hug and not too hard so I feel like I'm being winded. She releases me back onto the ward and I don't know what to do with myself. I sit on my bed and try to reflect on what Dr B has said. I have been given permission to sleep and ask people to do more with Arthur so that's what I'll have to do. Trust the process, trust it. It's all very odd, feeling like you are going from having to do everything to doing nothing.

After a deep breath and with a mini spring in my step after having been given some boundaries, I feel brave, so I head to the TV room. The instant I get in there, I regret it but being British, I sit down and just smile like an idiot at the whole room. I'm pretty sure I said 'Hi' but it was so faint, no one would have heard me. The Cool Kid of the ward, Room 2, is in there. Her boyfriend is here most of the time and he is today. They hang out in the lounge, eating biscuits and playing Scrabble. I realise I'm still too new for the lounge. She is funny, knows all the staff by name and seems to know how the place runs so I will need to get to know her, but this isn't the time. I quietly get up and scuttle out.

I go to the only place I'm comfortable in other than my room and it's the crèche. In there, I meet the reason the alarm went off the first night. She looks a similar age to me (I'm pleased about this; I seem to be the oldest mum in here). She simply and openly tells me that she just decided to take all the pills she had been hoarding in her room. A nurse had found her slumped during one of her checks and raised the alarm, hence the noise of running down the corridor.

'Yeah, sorry about that, that was me,' she says dismissively.

'Gosh, are you okay?' I question, not really knowing if I should be asking but she replies, seemingly quite happily, 'Yes, I'm fine, I've been over in the hospital for a few days.

Pretty convenient being next door!' she jokes. I can't help myself, so I blurt out, 'But how did you do it? I thought this place was pretty kill-yourself proof?'

'I'd been hoarding drugs in my room. I just pretended to swallow them when they gave me them. I then just decided that night was the right night and I took them all. I've done it before and I'm sure I'll do it again. My personality is just very impulsive like that. No planning (apart from hiding the drugs of course).' I'm a little shocked, I can't believe she just decides to 'do it' every so often, like it's nothing, not permanent.

She's very humble and intelligent so I can't understand why she overdoses. She can't remember how many times she's done it because it's so frequent, but I learn she has a compulsive disorder which means she can be fine one minute and then, in a split second, she decides to do something very rash. She has been here for nearly three months so has loads of knowledge of different kinds of medications and treatments I may or may not receive. I like her and I think I'll be pals with her if she wants to be pals with me. Phew, maybe I have the beginnings of a gang forming.

After all the excitement of the morning, I lie down to sleep after lunch. A siesta – they are allowed – but shortly after my head hits the pillow, a nurse knocks to tell me that Richard and Louise are here. 'Oh, okay', I say, 'I'll be down in a minute.' But I just stay, motionless on the bed. I can feel my eyes closing again and I know I have to drag myself out of this. Another ten minutes pass and I know I need to get up, but I just can't. I don't know if it's embarrassment or if I'm just so exhausted but I can't drag my body off the bed. The next thing I know, another hour has gone past and I figure they must have gone home.

I know I'm a terrible daughter-in-law, but I justify it to myself by thinking that they would have got to see and play with Arthur and that's what I'm sure they would have come for. They can keep up with how I am doing through Rhys. They didn't need to see the sorry state of me as well.

Sammy appears at the crèche door and tells us it's dinner time. It's actually 17:00 so it's certainly dinner time up north but since I've moved south, I'm lucky if I get dinner before 20:00. And don't get me started on supper. Supper is not dinner where I'm from. Supper is a piece of angel cake and a glass of chocolate milkshake where I'm from. And while we're at it, the meal in the middle of the day is lunch. End.

Everyone goes up to the hatch, says their room number, gets issued with a plate and then sits down and stares at their food.

Everything inside me wants to make conversation because that's what I do, but this is such an unusual situation, I'm not sure what's 'allowed'. There are also staff, HCAs, in the dining room (including mine) who have to follow some of the patients around full time due to the watch level they are on. I don't know if I can have a normal conversation with them or, because they are working, I'm not supposed to chat. Much like distracting a guide dog when it's with its owner and has a harness on. Suicide Lady, I'm learning, never eats in the dining room. She either gets her stuff and goes straight to her room or, if there is nothing she fancies, she goes hungry or a visitor will go and get her something. The Beautiful Girl, Room 8, has decided to sit with us today rather than returning to her room. She's painfully shy and I have learned that she's in here with her second child. Rape has brought this child into the world, rape set up by her ex-boyfriend. I'm speechless when I find out, speechless.

I take a deep breath and go for it: 'How did ward round go for everyone?' I say, looking at no one in particular. No one says a thing for what seems like ages and then thank goodness for Dark Glasses I met on the first day. She tells me that we are all being experimented on and that ward round is for them to gauge how the experiments are going. Interesting, I'm not sure where to go with this but I definitely want to hear more. I ask her how she's come to be here, to be a guinea pig.

One day she was gardening with her family and her husband was annoying her, so she threw a plant pot at his head. The husband called the police and she was taken in for questioning. She says it was there that they assessed her and thought she was a candidate to be experimented on; she had to come straight here from the cells. I ask why she had to bring her son with her. They are doing experiments on him too, apparently. I'm not really sure how to respond to this so I just nod and decide it's probably best if we all just eat our dinner in silence. I don't think anyone else was listening anyway.

21ST AUGUST

I'm minding my own business in my room, trying to make having a shower and getting ready take as long as possible when a nurse comes and asks me if I want to join the residents' meeting. 'Yeah. Sure, thanks.'

We all congregate in the TV room and I recognise most of the faces in there and take this opportunity to have a better look at everyone and try to catch the odd smile when anyone looks up. The nurse leading the meeting starts by reminding everyone when visiting hours are and asks if we all know who our named nurses are. Yes, mine is Carly. There are two nurses called Carly and I don't know which one of those is actually mine, but I don't want to be the only one to say I can't remember the person I was introduced to a matter of days ago so I leave it, figuring it will become clear as time goes on.

She then moves on to ask if anyone has any feedback about the meals. I'm about to launch into a little spiel about how grateful I am that I don't have to cook and that there was always something with custard to finish, when someone else starts to moan about cold chips. I realise I'm outnumbered so keep the thoughts to myself. Finally, we are asked if there is anything we'd like to do this coming week. No one volunteers anything so I decide it is my turn.

I know I have not been here that long, but I have been here for a weekend and I found it really quiet and it dragged. I suggest that we could maybe try to do a walk with the babies in their prams. If we are feeling super-brave and to give our walk purpose, we can maybe stop in an actual café for actual coffee. I see the staff looking at each other and nodding and Suicide Lady looks right at me, nodding, and I know then that she is actually my first hospital pal! I like that she's gone from Suicide Lady to Helen. She's my hospital buddy, Helen, and I feel far less alone knowing that.

As I'm leaving the meeting, a nurse pulls me aside to have a word. What on earth could this be? What have I done wrong? Maybe no one is supposed to say anything at that last bit of the meeting? I follow her to my room and she tells me that because I have been doing well with Arthur, they are taking me 'down a level'. Okay. Apparently, I won't have someone with me all the time now, they will just check on me every 15 minutes. Okay. Thinking about it, I haven't thought about killing myself once since I have been here. So, without knowing it, I have been on suicide watch and satisfied them I'm not going to do anything. Well done me.

Ellie visits this afternoon and I tell her my good news. She's pleased for me; she's always pleased for me. Goodness knows what I'd do without her.

22ND AUGUST

Rhys is visiting later. I'm not excited. Maybe I will be when it gets closer to the time. I hope so.

It's even closer to the time. I know he's left work and I'm still not excited. Oh God, what does this mean, do I not love him any more?

When he arrives at my door, thank goodness all I want to do is hug him. He looks knackered, his eyes are black, and I just feel deeply, deeply sorry for him. I ask him what his week has been like. He lies and tells me he's been productive at work. My heart breaks for him, what have I done to him? I've turned him into a shell of a man.

It's dinner time, he tells me to go but I don't want to leave him. He insists.

When I get back, he's lying on the play mat with Arthur. As I get closer, I realise their eyes are closed and they are both fast asleep. At first, I think he's playing around but as I say his name and he doesn't even flinch, I know he's asleep. I can't believe how tired he must be to have fallen asleep on a cold wooden floor, when in charge of his baby. Rather than feeling sorry for him, which I know is the feeling I should feel, I'm mad. I'm mad because I'm selfish. I know he's only here for a short time and during that time I want to actually do something with him, as opposed to him just sleeping it away. It's not enough for me to just have him here, he needs to bring the fun.

I decide to let him sleep as he'll only be grumpy if I wake him up. I lie on my bed and text Mum. I realise I've not really been in touch with her that much but it's not really like that much has happened. She's obviously pleased to hear from me. I tell her I'm having a pedicure tonight with an ex-patient and she remarks how wonderful that is for me. She always wants things to be wonderful.

I can't wait to meet the ex-patient. I put Arthur to bed and roam around the corridor waiting for her to appear. When she does, I'm pleased to get a slot with her. I don't care about my nails, I just want to talk to someone who has come out of the other end. Apparently, the ward called her to let her know how excited I was that she's coming. She obviously recognises me as the keen bean.

I peruse the colours, I'm not sure I like any of them. That's not the point, Canty, just pick any colour, you just want to get into the serious chat. I still can't make decisions and ask her to pick one she hasn't used in a while for me. As I sit back on the chair, she asks me all sorts of questions about how I feel, when I started to feel like this, how long I've been here and so on. I tell her but I really just want to get to the bit where I can grill her. I realise she might be asking me all of the questions so she can tell me how long she thinks I'll be here, what therapies they will try me on, so I just go with it.

When I get to ask her why she was here, she tells me about her complicated illness and I figure I'm going to have a totally different experience from her. I can't believe how complex her illness was and I'm shocked when I hear she was here for months, as opposed to weeks. *Oh yikes, I'm not sure I want to hear any more!* But there is something quite intriguing about hearing other people's journeys through motherhood, maybe it's not sweetness and light for more people than I thought. There are people roaming around in actual life, in the actual world, who also have distressing stories to tell about when they were new mums.

I get into bed, careful not to smudge my new sparkly nails, and remember that we are cooking with Anika, a nursery nurse, tomorrow. She was going to get all the ingredients on her way home after her 12-hour shift. How hard these people work for us, not only when they are on shift, is mind blowing.

23RD AUGUST

I see Anika walking into the office with a bag bulging with aubergines. I'm excited but I think it's because we are actually going to do something that's not sleeping. I can't believe that every time I put my head down, I sleep.

It's cooking time. I love an aubergine. We rarely have them at home as Rhys thinks they taste like slugs.

When we get into the kitchen, all of the drawers and cupboards are locked. Anika goes and gets the keys and explains this is a shared kitchen for all the wards. As I have been outside only a handful of times, I'd not really realised about the other wards in the same building. Apparently, we have the deaf guys and girls with diagnosed mental illness above us and those with eating disorders below us. That makes sense, I have seen a couple of ghost-like waifs when I've been out of the front door. Dark Glasses is often dancing with a chap who just makes noises when she's having a smoke. That makes sense now. What a relationship: she can jibber away as much as she likes and he just dances around to no music at all, nodding and smiling, a match made in heaven.

Anika comes back, releases all the sharp knives and dangerous blunt objects and pops a CD on. She then has us all doing a job. I like this, I like having something to do, I must have something to do. The other girls are pretty quiet, but we work well as a team, following Anika's instructions. I like Anika, she always needs to be busy. She reminds me of Normal Laura and I really hope that Normal Laura and Anika can meet in the future.

As we wheel our goods back to the ward, I'm pretty impressed with what we have made. I can't have the recipe as it's just out of Anika's head, she's been making curries since before I was born! I send a photo of my achievements to Rhys and he replies with a photo of him and Alma. He is smiling but they look sad.

On my phone, I see someone from my Cheltenham doctor's surgery is calling. I debate not picking up but it's the doctor's surgery, so I have to. Apparently, it was supposed to be Arthur's 12-week injections today and I have missed the appointment. Nooooo, now I'm one of those people on the NHS's blacklist. I grovel with the mental-hospital excuse and they are very understanding. They tell me not to worry about the timing and just book an appointment locally when I can.

I tell the nurses immediately and they tell me not to panic, they are on it. So I don't panic. Just before I go to leave their office, one of the nurses lets me know that I am now off 15-minute checks. What does this mean? Basically that someone will just have eyes on me every couple of hours and that if I need something, I am to ask.

24TH AUGUST

Ellie and Becca came today. I feel so guilty they are spending their weekends in this place with me. I'm here but they don't need to be.

I guess they feel they have a duty, but they never make me feel like that. It looked like rain but with my newfound freedom, I suggested going for a walk. I checked it was okay with the nurses, answered my two questions correctly (how I'm feeling and how long I think I'll be) and we were off.

I showed them the main hospital and pointed out all the chaps smoking with IV lines hanging out of their arms. I regurgitated the rumour that I have heard that most of Birmingham's drug deals happen outside the Queen Elizabeth hospital. I don't know if it's correct but it seems plausible and it's a good tale.

As we got to the university, the heavens opened. We looked at each other, laughed and legged it to the entrance of one of the university buildings. Arthur was mainly dry and still asleep in the sling and we all shook our heads, trying to get the wet off our hair.

As we were there, we took a little look around. It made me think about my university life. I look back on it mainly with fond memories. I'm sure there were boring bits when I was stuck in revising, but the brain has an amazing way of blocking those bits out. I hope my brain will have blocked this bit out when I look back on Arthur's childhood.

We watched the students run in from the rain and I felt for them, I wouldn't do university life again. I'm lucky I was able to go to university, I'm lucky that my physics teacher pushed me towards mechanical engineering and I got accepted. I'm lucky that I liked studying and got a good degree. I'm lucky to have a good job and to be able to provide for us.

The girls went and Rhys has come for the evening to do baby massage. One of the nursery nurses is studying it to offer on the ward and I am keen. I'm keen to do anything. I want to be able to try to look forward to stuff and to keep busy so the days go quicker and I don't have to spend more time wasting the days with sleep.

There are three of us at baby massage. I wonder what the others are doing and what the appeal of their rooms is. Maybe I need to jazz up my room a bit.

We undress the babies and I'm a bit surprised when the nurse instructs us to take their nappies off. The instant the baby girls' bits hit the fresh air, they start leaking, apparently, not that Rhys or I realise. Arthur is still holding strong. I cover Rhys in a towel, imagining the drama if Arthur were to wee.

Arthur seems to enjoy it; he smiles and it's lovely for me to see him and Rhys together.

Then Arthur starts pooing. It had to happen – relaxed, no nappy, what's a boy to do? I obviously take photos from all angles while Rhys rolls his eyes and asks for some wipes. I know he's enjoyed the session too.

25TH AUGUST

We go for our coffee today and it is quite a comedy. I find I have to laugh at a lot of things that happen in here otherwise I'd cry. I am ready with my pram and so is my new buddy, Helen. Getting the pram and bag ready has been less of a drama since I've been here. I can't believe how stressful I used to find it, so much so that I'd just risk flying by the seat of my pants and not even looking what was in the bag, I was so terrified of it. I had told the nurses pretty much on the first day that the randomness of when the baby wants to feed and nap was the number one thing that stressed me out the most. They asked if I would like to try scheduled feeding. I could have cried and hugged everyone in the room I was so overjoyed that this was a thing and that someone was going to help me with it. So we agree to go for coffee just after Arthur has had his first feed, although it is pretty much at the same time as Helen's son will need a feed. But she is happy to feed him outside of the unit – something I aspire to.

We are introduced to our allocated HCA, who is tasked with the responsibility of getting us to a coffee shop and back. She asks us where we want to go and if we want her to cover up her uniform. I speak for the both of us, saying to leave her uniform showing so when it all goes wrong, at least everyone will know we are from the mental hospital and they will give us a wide berth.

We head towards Harborne and manage to decide to go to the Boston Tea Party as Helen has been there before. So far so good, but when we get there, the café is pretty busy. This normally wouldn't be a problem, but you now have two anxious people who really need a coffee to complete their mission and nowhere obvious for them to sit. After standing in the middle of the café just staring at each other for what seems like a good ten minutes, a table over the far side becomes available. By the time we have moved all of the furniture to get our tank-like prams over, a table outside becomes available, so we plough our way back there.

I then become very aware that we are with a lady in uniform and immediately regret my decision for her not to cover it up. I can feel people staring at us and I must be crimson. Fair enough, if there are two people with two buggies causing havoc in a coffee shop accompanied by a nurse, I'd probably stare. After what seems like a lifetime, we both decide what we want and are then able to wind the anxiety levels down a little and make polite small talk about suicide and, you know, other casual coffee-time subjects.

When I get back to my room, I look at my phone and see a message with a photo attached from a friend. It's of three dogs: two are hers, the other is Alma. I understand they are going to look after her for a while as Rhys is working and driving up and down to Birmingham and sometimes staying over, so it's for the best.

All I can think of is poor Rhys rattling around in the house on his own – no Laura, no baby, no dog. Not exactly what he imagined his life as a new dad would be. He says he's all right and sends me a photo of the gates he's been building for our garden. I love him so much. He's like me, well, the old me – just keeps going and keeps himself busy.

He knows I'm a scaredy cat. Since finding a robber on my bedroom carpet in the middle of the night when I lived in Sydney, I've found it hard to have a night alone in a house. It took me a good few years to even be able to stay in a house with only one front door (as opposed to a flat in a block with other people around and two doors to get through). He knows that having gates at the back, so it's harder for people to get into our garden, would make me smile and it does.

26TH AUGUST

I'm still giving the first bottle of the day to my designated HCA to give to Arthur. Every morning I tell myself that I will do it but every morning, once I've changed his nappy, someone has appeared with a bottle, so I just give in to them and get straight back into bed. I can't believe I'm lucky enough to be here and to continue to be lazy. None of my friends who have had babies can do this; when their baby is up, they have to get up. I have the luxury of going back to sleep as someone else just does it for me.

A nurse wakes me up for my medication and I see a text from Rhys. It's a photo of what he's bringing today: mouthwash, sanitary towels, Sudacream and some exercise bands. I get up and make room on top of the sanitary bin for my mouthwash and figure the sanitary towels can go on the floor. I'm not sure how one could kill themselves with a small shelf but they must be able to as there isn't one in here. I asked the cleaning dude to antibac the top of the sanitary bin before it became my toiletries shelf and he seemed happy to do that.

When Rhys arrives, I find out that the bands have been very kindly sent up by Louise, bless her, she knows I've been saying I'm bored! I pop them on the desk and make a mental note to thank her.

27TH AUGUST

Ward round this morning – I cried again; I don't seem to be able to help it. I feel safe here. I don't think about killing myself and certainly not Arthur. But I still feel really low, really, really low and when I think about our future, all I can see is this big black space. A black space with no one in it and no enjoyment.

I got another hug afterwards from the nurse who walked me back to my room. Our chat gave me some hope and she then recommended I have a lie down, so I did and now I have taken a deep breath and have turned my mind to Ellie visiting this afternoon. That's what I'm focusing on.

Art and I meet Ellie off the train, casually. I just strapped on the baby carrier, asked the nurses if we could go and here I am meeting my friend off the train. There is a nurse loitering about twenty metres away but hey, on the face of it, it looks like I'm not a loon. I introduced Ellie to her, but she shook her head and insisted on hanging back. I really want to tell her it's okay, I really don't have any shame and it's probably less weird if she walks with us, but I can't get that across. It looks like we are now the normal ones being stalked by a crazy lady in a nurse's uniform.

Ellie has gone home and it's evening. I wander out of my room in my pyjamas. I've put on weight since I've been here, so my pyjamas look like they belong to my younger, skinnier sister. Suddenly I recoil. There's a very handsome man sitting right outside the door of Room 8. Right outside it. I panic and scurry back in, giving myself a quick look in the mirror. I look worse than I've ever looked in my life and I'm in a mental hospital, but I throw on my dressing gown and saunter out. 'You all right?' I say, nonchalantly. Hot Man mumbles back, so I stupidly ask him if he's going to be looking after Arthur tonight. He says he's the HCA for Room 8, actually, so I say, 'Cool' and casually wander down to the TV room. When I get there I immediately text Bec and El to tell them I've still got it.

28TH AUGUST

This time when Rhys comes to visit, I'm determined to do more than lie on my bed and let him fall asleep. I know it's probably all he wants and all he needs but I want to have a nice time. I'm pretty bored every day so I want time with him to feel special and different. I ask the nurses what time Costa closes and apparently it's late. Great, we can have a super-romantic date at Costa in the Queen Elizabeth Hospital.

When he arrives, it's nearly 17:00, so dinner time for me. I go to the dining room right at the end of dinner service and ask if Sammy has any spares. She's the loveliest and pops an extra potato and a huge dollop of beans on my plate. I walk the twenty metres back to my room feeling super-naughty.

Rhys can't believe I have asked for extra. Evidently, his usual rebellious attitude doesn't extend to taking an extra potato from the NHS.

Once we have finished our illicit dinner, I ask Rhys if he fancies a walk before Arthur's bathtime. His mouth says yes but his body language says no. But he's actually said yes so we're going.

It's a beautiful evening and as we get closer to the hospital, I can see a few police cars out the front. Oooo, interesting, we'll have front-row seats too. I love any documentary or fly-on-the-wall thing if it's to do with the police, hospitals or prison – they are all right up my street. Rhys just wishes I'd stop staring but I can't help it, I've been asleep for most of the day. I get in the queue at Costa to order and the lady in front of me has her leg in plaster and can't stay still. I'm just debating how to ask her if she knows what's been going on outside when she turns around and asks me if I can believe it. 'Believe what, love?' I let a bit of northern out, I feel like it bonds us as she has a strong accent.

It turns out that she's front and centre of said drama. She was in A&E having her leg seen to with her boyfriend earlier on today. He then went out for a cigarette and some lads started on him (allegedly). He's now in theatre having a knife wound seen to. Errr, yikes, I wanted to know but I don't know if I want to be any part of this now. She's so into telling me that she's not answering the Costa man behind the counter. I keep trying to butt in, but she can't stop. She's understandably livid and I imagine pretty pissed off the attention isn't on her and her broken leg, it's now all about him and the fight.

With that, someone shouts something from the revolving doors and she's off, as fast as she can be on her crutches. It sounds like there is another battle to be fought on the QE frontier. Hot chocolate with marshmallows and a side of knife crime. (Seriously, I hope the bloke is okay.)

It's been nice, I think I've enjoyed it. I don't feel anything inside, still, but I think that's okay. I'm pleased we went out but I'm not sure it was the right thing to do for Rhys. He looks more tired than ever and I worry about him making it back along the motorway to bed. When we get back to the unit, he asks if I mind if he gets off and leaves me to bath Arthur. Now I know it wasn't all right. I totally don't mind, and I'm quite pleased he's asked. Maybe now, finally, for the first time in a long time, it's not all about me.

30TH AUGUST

I wake up anxious. My friend Jill (Holly's mum) is coming to visit today and I've not seen her since I was totally nuts in Cheltenham. I know she's been thinking of me and I know she's desperate to help so I want her to think I'm doing a bit better.

When I get dressed, I notice more than ever that my jeans are getting tight and some T-shirt sleeves are starting to dig into my arms. I pop the tightest pair of jeans in the case under my bed, so I don't have the disappointment of putting them on and realising how tight they are again.

Jill arrives looking glamorous and smelling delicious and I'm more embarrassed than ever to be in the hospital. She's keen to see what the place is like as she's been a nurse and a health visitor in her former life, so I guess this is doubly interesting for her.

The last time I went for lunch with her I was a jabbering idiot. I remember us walking to Bath Road (Alison was with Arthur at home) and she remarked how wonderful the lavender smelled. What? Who cares about lavender and why is she even mentioning it? I remember that even annoyed me, flipping lavender. The place we went to and our conversation is a bit of a blur now, but I remember not knowing what to order so she took charge and ordered for me. When she sat down, I remember just spilling everything to her. How much I hated it, how much conflicting advice I was getting. I remember not being able to sit still and not wanting to eat anything, but I had to as she'd been kind enough to get it for me. I remember I was wearing fisherman pants, as they felt comfy on my tummy, and a feeding top that really could have done with a wash. I remember Arthur had been sick on it that morning but I didn't have any other clean ones, so I'd done my best to get rid of the smell with baby wipes. And there I was, sat in a café where I wouldn't normally be seen dead without my makeup on.

This time, however, I don't look like the great unwashed and I definitely don't look like a hippy. I've not worked up to makeup and hair straighteners yet, but I have a small baby and I have at least clean hair and clothes and that's okay.

I go and order lunch for us at the café, totally casually, like I've always been able to do that. As soon as the food arrives, Arthur starts crying. I'm not panicked, I simply lift him out of his pram and feed him his bottle. We're having salad, it's not going to go cold. As I support his chin in one hand and expertly shovel food in my mouth with the other hand, Arthur falls asleep and Jill just can't believe it.

I'm not the same person she saw last time. I think this is the first time I realise I've actually made some progress.

31ST AUGUST

My phone bings and it's a photo on the antenatal class WhatsApp group of all the babies together at a baby group. I've been keeping up to date with the messages, kind of, but I've not replied to anything as I just don't feel part of it any more. They have done absolutely nothing to deserve that. They have been nothing but amazing with me. As soon as they all heard about my diagnosis, they rallied round and sent me a hamper full of delicious eats, drinks and bath things. How amazing, right? Eight strangers put together only because they are due to have a baby at the same time and live in vaguely the same area. One couple has dropped off but seven still sticking together is pretty remarkable.

I think back to the times we used to go to that baby group together at the local church. There was always a flurry of messages that morning as to who was going and who couldn't make it or, more commonly, messages professing enthusiasm to get there this week and then, inevitably, not being able to make it at the last minute. The baby group started at 11:15 so at about 10:45 I'd be thinking about what I'd need, what I should leave at the house, willing him to have a feed at home so I didn't have to feed him there. I'd pace for a lot of the build-up and then decide it was time to leave the house at about 11:00, giving me 15 minutes to walk the hundred metres down the road to the church.

I'd inevitably be the first there and when the lady asked me if I'd like a drink and a piece of cake, I could always feel my eyes fill with tears. I didn't know if the lady who ran it was a volunteer from church or if it was a business, but she was kind, smiley and had time for everyone. She made the most amazing cakes and we'd all sit around the edge of the room, our babies laid in front of us like potatoes with arms and legs. There would be loads of toys and sensory bits in the middle of the circle for us to help ourselves to.

I'd look at the other girls, my new pals, and my mind would chatter at me. *She looks stunning, how has she managed that, oh good, she still has wet hair, I know I look like shit but I think that's okay, not everyone has makeup on, baby on the left has just puked, good, it will be okay if Arthur does, shall I feed him, is that just a grumble or is it a cry, please don't escalate, please don't…*and on and on it would go. I would ask how the other girls were and then ask them endless questions that usually started with, 'How do you know...' There was always a 'speaker' and this person could range from someone advertising their baby group to someone from the local council supporting reusable nappies.

I will always remember the first session as it was a very enthusiastic lady, probably my age, with an amazing voice. She introduced a life-size doll to us that was her baby for the purposes of the session. She then launched into songs, while moving various things over the doll's face. I couldn't take my eyes off her face. She was beautifully made-up and she didn't stop smiling, even when she was singing. Every word was beautifully enunciated and she made sure she looked at every mum in the room and every baby. I looked at the other girls – they had the same massive grins on their faces, looking at their babies and doing the same actions at the teacher. They looked so happy, they were so in the moment, so engaged, so wanting their little ones to respond to the massive amounts of effort they were putting in.

I'd looked at Arthur and thought, *he doesn't care about this, he doesn't want to be laid on this stranger's mat kicking his arms and legs about and having stuff jammed in his face*. Once I had assessed all the mums there, my mind was consumed by my old life. Only a few short months before, I was working in the Middle East. I was teaching cyber-security courses to a load of military folk whose life ambition was to serve their country and keep it safe from cyber attacks. I'd have conversations with guys who had spent their lives dedicated to their country, who had palatial offices with televisions four times the size of mine. I'd have to build rapport with guys from a totally different culture from mine. And I'd had a team working for me, expecting me to know what I was doing, direct them, support them, develop them and care for them when they were so far from home. And now, here I was with a chiffon scarf, listening to a lady who could have been famous with that voice, but she was here, in a church in Cheltenham with a life-size doll. But she is happy with that and my new mum pals are happy, they wouldn't want to be anywhere else right now.

And I wasn't in the room, I was never in the room, I was always thinking about what I used to do and how far removed from it this was.

I bring my mind back to the photo on my phone. I look at all the babies one by one. I look at how much they have changed, and I realise how long it's been since I've seen them. We've all been through the mill one way or another – babies not sleeping, tongue tie, unknown allergies, colic, broken fannies, falling-off nipples, losing our minds – you name it, we have had it. I message them to say I'm doing okay, that I hope they all are too and that I hope to see them soon. One by one they all reply. What a bunch of great human beings.

I'm sad Arthur isn't in the photo with them but when I think about being at home, it still scares me to death. We're just having different maternity leaves. Mine is here in this odd computer game and theirs is there. Sometime soon, they will come together.

After visiting me, Rhys gets to his hotel and I ask him how bad it is. I hope he's lucked in but sadly not, I think he sleeps fully clothed. I wish he could stay with us. I wish there was a wing for partners. I don't want to be in a bed with him as I'm just getting this sleeping thing down. And I want to do my own thing in the morning but I wish he didn't have to pay his hard-earned money to stay in a dump and all because of me.

He's got his cricket final tomorrow, so he needs sleep to ensure he's on top form. They have to win. After all this, they have to.

CHAPTER 7

THE TURNING POINT

2ND SEPTEMBER

The girls text to ask me if I want them to bring anything. Normally it's a 'just you', but this time I know what I want.

Bring my makeup, please. I think Canty is starting to make a return and she needs to be looking less slug-like.

It's been so long since I have worn any makeup I cannot tell them exactly what I would like. It appears they have got to my house within about five minutes and they are sending me photos of stuff, asking yes or no. I'm surprised at every photo. 'That's mine? I own that? Ooooo, I'd forgotten about that.'

I realise that's the call they have been waiting for and all of me is so pleased to have made it. I just ask them to bring what they think. Anything I don't want, Rhys can take back home with him later on. I'm going to enjoy going through the parcel when it arrives, even if it is all just my stuff!

I can't wait for them to arrive. I miss them. I want to be alive and I want to enjoy life and I can't imagine never seeing them again. Friends make the world go around. There are things you share with friends that you don't share with your partner, there are things friends know about you that no one else does or ever will. They are there for you in the good times and they will hang on through the bad times as they know how good the good times are and they know they will return. I can't believe I moved to Cheltenham initially knowing no one and how lucky I have been to have met some amazing, loyal, kind people. They are friends through a variety of things – work, friends of friends, the gym, housemates, nearly housemates – and when I think of them all individually, they all give me something to live for.

When Bec and Ellie arrive, I'm so excited to see them. We make a bee line for the exit and go to my favourite coffee shop. On the walk there, Rhys texts to say he's ten minutes away and where should he come to. I like that he's had to call and ask, I'm not just always in my room any more, I've started to get a taste of what maternity leave 'should' look like. Rhys arrives with his big smile, his team won and he's as happy as ever to see Arthur. As he's cuddling his son and we're all still looking at the menu, I suddenly get a feeling of fear running through my veins. It's all just going a bit quick. I'm out with my friends and Rhys and we're all chatting, and I have makeup on and I look non-crazy. Is that it? When I get back, are they going to turf me out?

Rhys goes to order for us all. When he asks what we want, we all say some kind of coffee; he seems disappointed as he's going for a burger with everything. I immediately look at the menu and it's £17.50. The fear grows. We have no money. We've just spent loads on the house and now I'm making him spend even more travelling up and down here, and the petrol, it will all be adding up.

I just take a listening role, my head is away, spinning, mulling things over, coming up with solutions but then working out why they won't work. The girls and Rhys chat, I think I answer some questions and then we all walk back to my bedroom. As we get there, I have a Sunday blues feeling wash over me. I get the feeling everyone else does too. They are in a city they don't work in and in less than 24 hours they have to be at work. I know they will be leaving soon and I can't keep it in any longer. I burst into tears. I feel immediately guilty. As if it's not enough that you are in a mental hospital, you've now started crying. Can you ever make it not about you, Laura?

When I get called for dinner, I walk them to the door. As I watch them walking along the corridor, chatting, I can feel the tears brimming again. They can walk away. I can't. They will be in their houses tonight, they have lives outside of here. My life is here and what a waste it is. I just hope someone pressed the pause button when we left home so we can just step back into life after this game is over.

As I sit down with a sad-looking plate, just waiting for it to be okay for me to have pudding and custard, my dad texts. *Wrong time, Dad,* I think, *you're about to get a stream of consciousness.* He does. I tell him how I'm worried about Rhys. I know I'm the one making him this tired, this stressed and this down-beaten but I can't do anything but trust the process and that doesn't come with a time scale. I'm worried Rhys and Arthur's relationship is going to be affected. I'm worried he's having to spend what little money we have travelling up and down to Birmingham and on awful hotels where he doesn't get a good night's sleep. I tell Dad I can't imagine what it's like for him being home alone and I don't know how on earth he is coping.

This time will pass, he tells me. I wish we could un-pause and press fast forward.

3ʳᵈ SEPTEMBER

I've just had ward round. I couldn't hold it together again. I can't imagine how I'm affecting these students and I don't know why they come back for more. I have definitely ensured there will be fewer babies in the world than there might otherwise have been. They would be mad to have one after hearing all this.

Dr B has had enough, he's going to make a radical change to my drugs. The hope is gone that Citalopram will work. What an absolute bugger, I've been on them for weeks just hoping they would kick in eventually. He's positive that the switch onto a new family of antidepressants will be what I need, that and changing my sleeping tablets combined with staying on the Quetiapine. I'm going to spend the next few days weaning off the current ones, have a couple of days free of antidepressants, then I'll start on the new one, Venlafaxine, next week. They fully expect me to be all over the place – dizzy and emotional – and that I'm going to want to sleep a lot. No change there. Dr B finally tells me again to lean on the staff.

They have also booked me an appointment to have Arthur's round of jabs I missed in Cheltenham at the local surgery. And they will come with me. Okay, that should be okay.

I walk back to my room in tears again, knowing that the next week will be a write-off while I come off the very thing I thought was going to help me. I think back to when they handed me that packet of hope, all that time ago, in my living room.

And I'm fat, I'm getting fat and it's not going to end any time soon with all these drugs going into me.

4TH SEPTEMBER

I'm feeling dizzy. Maybe it's in my head, maybe it's because I have reduced the dose of the thing that doesn't work. I'm sure this whole being-ill thing is in my head, so being dizzy because I know I've changed the dose of a drug may as well be too.

I decide today will probably be a day when I stay in bed most of the day. As I'm lying there with Arthur content in his bouncing chair, I get a text from Rhys with a photo taken in our bedroom of a bloke I don't know varnishing the door. My thoughts go straight back to that room, the room I lay awake in for hours and hours and hours on end.

It takes me a nanosecond to go from the bedroom to the ensuite. The room I had convinced myself was a better place to jump from. It was a floor higher than Arthur's room and I remember thinking that if I aimed for the paving stones below, I would definitely end it then. I remember being excited, not sad or scared, excited that this life would end. The only problem with that plan was how to get my wobbly, baby-ruined body through that tiny window.

I put the phone down and lie there, staring at the wall. I have spent a lot of time staring out of windows at pigeons and a lot of time staring at this wall next to my bed. As it's so close, it makes everything go out of focus, my brain gets even more confused and I start seeing circles appearing. It starts to hurt my eyes, so I turn over and look at the photo again. The doors are being varnished. Well, that was so far down the list I thought it would never come to the top. I remember thinking that they would get varnished with all Arthur's crayon marks included in about five years' time, if at all.

My heart is then suddenly proud. If Rhys has managed to arrange this, he must be okay. My Rhys, in the outside world, still just getting on with things knowing that the mother of his child, and his child, are in a mental hospital forty miles away for an undefined amount of time.

5TH SEPTEMBER

Still dizzy. I explain to the nurses I feel like I'm on a boat. I'm okay and I can get where I'm going, I just might not get there in a straight line and might have to grab something every now and then to save me from capsizing. Art has nursery time, so I take to my bed and think I'll just ride it out with some more sleeping.

I can't sleep but I figure being perfectly still is nearly as good, so I just lie down and stare and think. I think about running. When I was at home in Cheltenham, everyone would say to me, 'What do you enjoy doing?' And they would always suggest that perhaps I could go for a little run as I like running. Running was what I did. It was part of me. I'd run at the weekends, I'd run before work and I'd run to work. I'd enter things and it would make me feel good. It also seemed to counteract whatever I ate. I never worried about what I ate because I'd always run.

It didn't matter who suggested it – Bec, Kim, the Crisis Team – I just couldn't imagine putting a sports bra on, putting leggings on, tying my hair up, leaving the house. Why would I do that? I'd remind them of my always-there knee pain that had made me pull out of a few events in the past and they couldn't argue with that, could they? I know I would barely be able to run down the street so why would I want to set myself up to be disappointed? They would say that's not the point but that didn't matter to me. I would never enter a race if I knew I wouldn't beat the time I got in the same race the year before. I mean, I'm no athlete, we're not talking world records here, it's just me against myself. And I enjoyed it, it made me feel good.

But, now I'm here, I think I feel differently. I'm so fed up with being such a sloth and, now I'm not breastfeeding, there is a chance that my old sports bras might fit. I make a mental note that I'll ask Rhys to bring my running stuff. If it fits, I might be able to start running here and then when I get back into my actual life, I might be able to run the routes I used to before Arthur was born without having to stop and walk. I'm pretty fat now, which will make it harder but, actually, I might be able to lose some weight with running.

As I'm deep in thought, making a plan to get myself back to running, an HCA turns up at the door. She says there is a sensory class going on in the crèche and I might like to go and see Arthur joining in. Okay, thanks, I will. I'll take my phone too in case I want to take photos. In the crèche, I find Arthur sat on a ball, being held by an Occupational Therapist (OT). He has a smirk on his face; I want to take a photo to share with Rhys and Mum, so I do. And then I take another.

Next out of the OT's box of tricks comes a big blow-up fish. Arthur starts to cry, and I find myself wanting to hug him and tell him it's okay. The fish goes away and he calms down. Then there are flashing light balls all over the crèche and he doesn't know where to look.

And then I hear it come out of me.

That voice I heard all the girls doing at that baby class at the church. That enthusiastic voice of a mum trying to show her offspring something new and, at the same time, reassure them it's not scary. 'It's okay, Arthur,' I hear myself say, with a reassuring hand on his back. And for a moment, I am that person. The person I should have been months before. I cared about Arthur seeing the balls and I didn't want him to be scared of the fish. I wanted to take photos of him with different expressions on his face, experiencing new things. I wanted to document that and share it with people.

This is new.

6TH SEPTEMBER

The boat feeling seems to be even more boat-like today. The pills have changed over the last few days so the new tablet is getting into my blood and into my brain.

Rhys arrives just after lunch with a carrier bag stuffed full. I take it from him to my room and tip everything out on the bed. Wow, there is stuff I have not seen for years. One pair of leggings I remember, and I put them in the keep pile. He's also brought a shock-absorber sports bra and a T-shirt which claims I ran the Brighton Marathon in 2014. The T-shirt is white and the bra black. Men. He urges me to try them on as he takes Arthur to the garden.

The leggings fit! They are Lycra so it would be hard for them not to. Next, I try the sports bra. As I pull it around my chest and look down to do the clasp up, I can't believe how far off fastening it I am. It's probably a good couple of inches. I pull hard and I do it up. I twist it into place and pull the straps up, nearly dislocating my shoulders doing the extra clasp across my shoulder blades. I can't believe how tight it is but at least I can still breathe. I'm not breastfeeding so, surely, they should be smaller. But I am putting on weight and I guess a lot of it is going here. A friend told me that your rib cage doesn't settle back to its 'normal' position until about nine months after birth. I thought she was just saying it to be nice, which she probably was, but I'll go with it for now. After I pull on the relatively baggy (it's always been baggy) T-shirt, I dare to look in my plastic, very non-flattering but suicide-proof mirror and I look okay.

In fact, I think I look more than okay. The T-shirt hides the bulges of my bra but I'm focusing on my thighs and I think they look, dare I say it, *thin*. My thighs have always been my 'problem area' so this is awesome. I want to show Rhys as I think he might think I look good too but the garden is all the way down the other end so people will definitely see me. I take a deep breath and can feel my cheeks colouring up as I open my bedroom door and step out.

As I step into the garden, he looks twice and says I look great. I knew I wasn't dreaming it! I can't quite believe it. Not only do my pre-baby running bits fit, but I actually look okay in them. Maybe I was so depleted in calories that eating like a horse since I have been here hasn't caught up with me yet. This is amazing. I pop my tracksuit bottoms back on and tell myself that I'm going running tomorrow.

As I get into bed, I put the running bits on the high-backed purple chair at the end of my bed. This was a trick I used to use at home. There was more shame in putting the running stuff, unused, away in the cupboard than putting it on and not going very far or very fast.

7TH SEPTEMBER

I think I'm pleased with myself. I think that feeling overrides the one of guilt for leaving Arthur. I did it. I got up, put the running gear on and as soon as I stepped outside my room, the nurses and HCAs were asking me if I was going for a run. 'Well, errr, yes, would that be okay? Would someone be able to look after Arthur, please? I'm sure I won't be long.' They seemed to trip over themselves in a hurry to get to the office to confirm with the nurse in charge today that I could. It was cleared, he had about three people looking after him and I was allowed to go.

I had noticed a canal when I'd been walking so my plan was to head there, try to run for an amount of time along said canal and then turn and run back. As I got to the main front door, I smiled at the security guard and I think even he was taken aback. One of the mad mums was not only alone, but she was in Lycra and she was off. Outside, Dark Glasses was of course having a smoke with her best deaf pal, bopping away to the different tunes playing in each of their heads. They both gave me massive grins, Dark Glasses looked me up and down and I was convinced there was probably more than just tobacco in their cigarettes. I confidently strode towards the steps to get down to the canal, breathing deeply in a bid to try to warn my body what was about to happen.

When I got to the bottom of the steps, there were people running past in both directions, so I stood and waited. When the runner going the same way as me was a few metres past, I started running. I was putting one foot in front of the other, faster than I would if I was walking. Here I was, running. It felt a little bit jerky, like my knees were on backwards, but I was definitely not walking. As the person ahead of me slowly turned into a speck in the distance, I looked at my watch. I'd been running for four minutes. Jesus, this is why people give up. How on earth can that have only been four minutes? I told myself I was going to go to the next lamp post and then I could walk. I did. When I was walking, I strode like I had purpose. Every time someone overtook me, a little part of me died but I kept saying over and over *this is the first time you have run since having your abdomen cut open, that's seven layers of tissue, Laura, give yourself a break*. Still, I had my story of why I was walking planned in case anyone asked me if I was okay. I was a bit worried that I would start oversharing, but no one asked so that was a worry I needn't have had.

As I reached the next lamp post, I gave myself permission to turn around and go back. It was at this point that I suddenly realised how far away the steps were. I couldn't see them and they were definitely around a couple of bends. You idiot, why did you come this far? People who are not your friends or family are looking after your son while you do this, something for you. They could be doing something for them but no, they are having to

191

look after your boy because you want your old life back. The sooner you realise you are not going to get your own life back, Canty, the better.

I ran all the way back to the stairs in mild panic, the phrase 'I won't be long' repeating through my head. As I started walking up the steps, I felt like my heart was going to burst out of my chest and my backwards knees were going to give in. I gave myself permission to walk up the steps but then walking back towards the hospital seemed to be too slow so I started to jog as quickly as I could. By the time I was back outside The Barberry, Dark Glasses must have been on her tenth cigarette. As I got closer, she realised it was me and looked annoyed. She asked me why I didn't ask her to join me. I didn't know the answer, it had never crossed my mind. I'm sorry. We chatted while I got my breath back and agreed I'd let her know next time I was going. Off I went through the main doors.

The new security guard asked me who I was there to visit. I laughed and carried on walking towards the next door as he shouted after me. Oh, he wasn't joking, I thought he was trying to be funny or perhaps flirting a little. No, Laura, big head.

I told him I was a patient, but I'd been allowed out for a run as someone was looking after my baby. He thought about this for a few seconds and didn't say anything, so I carried on walking and this time he didn't shout after me.

I buzzed the door at The Chamomile Suite main entrance and waited for someone to answer. When they did, it was the nurse in charge that day and she walked down the corridor towards the door with a big grin on her face. 'How did it go?' she said. 'It was good, thanks. I wasn't that fast, and I didn't go that far but I wasn't totally useless and my scar didn't hurt too much.' I went on to tell her that I came back as I felt so guilty leaving Art. She tutted and told me not to be silly, all while smiling. She said it was important to get the balance right of being a mum but also having time for myself. And when I was back at home, Rhys would have Arthur if I wanted to go for a run. I consciously let this sink in. Once I got to the trio looking after Arthur, they told me what a dream he had been. I smiled with pride and kissed his chubby cheek. One of them then went to get me some fresh towels and told me to take a long hot shower and not to worry. For a brief, very brief, moment, I could have been in a spa.

So now, back in my room and showered, and thinking it all back through, I am proud of myself and when I do go home, I'll make sure I continue to get back into running.

My phone bleeps and it's Kim. Lovely Kim! I'm so pleased to get her message. I proudly tell her I've been for a run and I can imagine her reading the text and thinking *finally!*

After I've dried my hair and thanked my mum silently again for packing the dryer, I go to get Arthur and bring him back to my room for a bit before lunchtime. The new lady from next door pokes her head around the side of my door and asks if it was me who had the hairdryer and could she borrow it. Of course! I quickly unplug it and pass it to her like it was contraband.

Rhys is coming tonight and staying in another dodgy hotel. I'm quite looking forward to going to Costa, it's rapidly becoming our favourite haunt. We both like people-watching and guessing people's back stories. I think it also probably makes us feel like teenagers again. I just hope he's not too tired and can string a sentence together.

8TH SEPTEMBER

Rhys was dead on his feet last night, so we've arranged to go for breakfast this morning. It feels like we are dating again. But we have a baby. Weird, but hey, I'm going with it. We arrange to meet at the coffee shop we both have got to know, and I'm surprised when I turn up and he's there already. I love seeing him with Arthur but I can tell that he's still desperately tired and, despite telling me he slept well, I'm sure he didn't. We don't have to be talking all the time to prove to ourselves or anyone else that everything is fine. But sitting in silence I can't handle.

I need to start lowering my expectations. I'm not sure why I expect it's going to be like going on a first date again every time I see him. *It's not, a lot of water has passed under the bridge and you are in a mental hospital because you are ill. You are trying to go about doing normal things in a bid to get better, but you are still ill. You are both doing the best you can. Rhys is obviously going to be tired, and stressed and, let's face it, plain sad. He's trying to live his life knowing there are these massive parts missing. They are in Birmingham getting better and it's going to take some time. He can't just switch that off every time he comes to see us.*

The rest of the day, these thoughts go around and around and around in my head. Who is looking after Rhys?

9TH SEPTEMBER

Jenny and Kate came today. Kate is Bec's girlfriend and Jenny is a super-close friend so I know they have been asking after me. It was just so wonderful to see them. I played it safe and went to the same old café I was at yesterday with Rhys, but it's nice there and I know where I'm at. We laughed, a lot – how amazing is that? I feel like a bit of a fraud as I must seem like me. They must be wondering what I'm doing here, especially when they had the pleasure of seeing some of the new inmates on the ward.

One lady insists on putting a silk balaclava-type accessory on her child all the time. We all think it might be for some kind of religious reason. We would, of course, ask the mum but she has not spoken a word since she was admitted a couple of days ago. She just moves around like a ghost. Eating and staring a lot.

I still can't believe friends are travelling to see me, but they are. It makes it feel more like a weekend at home – friends, coffee, catching up. I guess many people don't have the opportunity to visit a pal in a mental hospital, I know I've always wondered what one is like.

10TH SEPTEMBER

We're upping the dose from tomorrow. At ward round this morning, Dr B and his entourage seem to be pleased that

Venlafaxine, despite my only having taken it for a few days now, seems to be working. I explain to them that I still feel like I'm on a boat every so often but I'm not crying in ward round because I think every day is worse than the one before, so that's good. My days are not on a linear trajectory up, but they are definitely not as bad as the first week I was here. Yes, that's a good thought, I can categorically say that no days this week have been worse than any of the days the first couple of weeks I was here. And I got through ward round without crying, excellent. I can't quite believe I'm about to hit the month mark, but I'm still a little terrified that they are going to send me home. I can't even process that in my head yet. My thoughts get as far as seeing the mud pit at the front of the house with the planks across it and I literally shake my head to make them go away. I have not yet pictured the inside of the house. Even writing the word 'house' is making me tingle.

I go to dinner for the usual chat about ward round and what everyone has been told they are stopping or starting to take. I ask opinions on Venlafaxine. A few have been on it and they can sympathise with the boat feeling. I tell them I'm going up to a higher dose and they all tell me that the dreams are going to get really weird. They already are. I'm not sure how much stranger they can get, but it could be fun. One of the girls tells me she had to come off it as the dreams were getting really dark. Oh, that doesn't sound fun at all.

One of the new girls tells me that her dad thinks I'm great and he's encouraged her to be on the same drugs as me, exactly the same. She gets out a pen and paper as he's told her to write them down and to tell the doctor that she wants exactly what I'm having. I'm a bit cagey but I figure telling her isn't going to do any harm. It's not like the doctor is going to just do what her dad says. He is pretty big, though. I never hear any more about it so assume it's probably just another one of those fleeting thoughts, along with having to give her dog to the dogs' home pretty much every other day while the days between are filled with going to get him out of the dogs' home. That poor dog. I hope she can work everything out. That poor girl, just doing what her brain tells her to do, day in, day out.

Dark Glasses is pouring yoghurt on her jam sponge and custard and telling us all how delicious it is and that we should get some. She has two mouthfuls and then bids us all good night.

They are crazies but they are my crazies, and I feel something for every single one of them.

Thank goodness Bec comes that evening and delivers a dose of normality to the place. We bath Arthur and put him into his cot before going to chat in the crèche. I ask her about work and about Kate and about Cheltenham and it's good to get a sense of what's going on outside my computer game. She's coming back to celebrate my birthday at the weekend with Ellie. I think I'm actually looking forward to something. Marvellous. I know she's not a hugger but, regardless, I hug her goodbye and knowing I'll see her again soon keeps the tears away, for me at least.

12ᵀᴴ SEPTEMBER

Last night was funny. Well, it wasn't funny at the time but it's making me smile thinking how ridiculous it was now.

After Bec had gone, I did my usual. Got ready for bed, took my drugs and read a few chapters of my book before I felt my eyelids droop, then turned off the light and rolled over. I must have drifted off straight away, only to be woken abruptly as my door flung open and Room 2 burst in.

'I need your help', she stated.

'Errr, hello, okay, yes, of course, what's up?' I asked in a bit of a daze, but now fully awake as she'd turned the light on.

'I'm going to court tomorrow and I have nothing to wear. I don't want to go super-smart, but I want to look like a sensible person who can look after a child.' Okay, I thought, I've not really had to consider what to wear to go to court to fight for my child, thankfully.

'Well, show me what you're thinking, you must have something', I said.

With this, she went back to her room and appeared in no time with an armful of clothes. She dumped them in the middle of my floor and it looked like a Blue Peter presenter had just thrown up. I have never seen so much colour, in contrast to my monochrome wardrobe.

'I mean your clothes, not your daughter's. I thought we were talking about you?' I questioned.

'They are my clothes', she replied, looking a tad confused.

'Of course, sorry', I said, sliding out of bed and kneeling next to the pile.

I realised then that we were in for a bit of a long night and we'd probably get told off for being in each other's rooms. But I wanted to help so we started trawling through the heap.

We ended up with something that looked sensible-ish. This included a cream cardigan of mine, some strict instructions not to smoke in it, and a firm promise that she wouldn't. Good luck, Room 2. You've got this.

Rhys arrives after dinner to do another baby-massage session. No pooing this time but plenty of wee flying around. He chats with the other girls and, apart from one of them having zero confidence AT ALL, it all seems relatively normal. It is nice.

Afterwards, as we are bathing Arthur, we hear a jubilant Room 2 running up and down the corridor shouting, 'We beat court, we beat court!' Rhys looks at me and asks what it's all about. I mention the episode last night and can only assume Room 2 will be going home soon with her daughter. Rhys tries to recall who this is, so I mention some of the other episodes – thinking she was possessed by the devil and locking herself in the laundry…threatening to cut all her hair off with some contraband scissors. He remembers and we carry on with the bedtime routine.

I must remember to get that cardigan back. The winning cardigan.

Mum is coming tomorrow.

13ᵀᴴ SEPTEMBER

I'm woken up by texts from Mum with her journey progress. This has always been a thing between us. She likes to let me know the puffer is puffing out of the station. I can't think of the number of texts we have shared with the word 'puffer' since I left home at 18. I know her excitement will be at fever pitch by the time she arrives. I get ready and go to the front to meet her. Of course, Dark Glasses and her deaf pal are outside, smoking themselves into a frenzy. It dawns on me that Mum is going to stare a lot today. Not that she means to stare, but I know she likes to take everything in. God knows how today is going to go but I'm quite looking forward to it.

As she steps out of the taxi, she wishes the driver luck for his upcoming wedding. My mum missed her calling as a spy. I swear she can find out anything about anyone within ten minutes. The cab journey can't have been more than about twenty minutes long and she can pretty much tell me the names and ages of all his children and what they are studying at school. In the nicest possible way, I do not care – illness or no illness!

I take her inside, and she of course cannot process a word I'm saying as she's looking around, taking everything in. I tell her this is just reception and that the fun really only begins when we get to my actual ward. I press the buzzer and Jan comes up the corridor to let us in. Before I know it, Mum's introducing herself as 'Laura's mummy', shaking her hand and launching into a speech thanking her so much for looking after Arthur and I. Jan looks at me mildly panicked so I give her a 'go with it, Jan, it will end eventually' nod and we carry on walking. I know Mum'll be hugging her and inviting her for a barbecue before the day is over.

It must take about 15 minutes to get to my room as Mum has to meet every member of staff and shake all their hands and thank them for looking after us on the way. They are all 'wonderful', as always, but so is she – she cares so much, and I know she will have been anticipating this day for so long.

She compliments one of the nurses on his earring. He smiles politely as I give him a 'sorry' look and I don't have the heart to tell her that that's the clip that holds his prosthetic ear on. It's at this point I realise I should have probably given her the heads up on all the staff and what to say and not to say but I didn't. We'll just have to see how that plays out. I put imaginary money on the fact that she will be finding out Sue's life story before long. She's one of the HCAs working today – she's a bit older and seems to love Arthur so I know we'll see her at some point. Her only son died in a car accident. He was in his teens. Thinking about it makes everything inside me ache with pain for her.

Once we are finally in Room 7, Mum marvels at how wonderful it is and how all my things have a place. Everything in my mum's life is wonderful. I can't help myself and point out there are no taps and no door handles so you can't hang yourself. This obviously isn't so wonderful, but she can see why, and we move on.

Judging by the volume of stuff Mum has with her, it looks like she's moving in, but as she starts to unpack, it's all the components of my birthday cake which she'll construct later. She encourages me to open my birthday presents, even though it's a few days away. I open a bright pink lipstick and a mascara and put the lipstick on immediately.

I switch things up for lunch and head to a tapas bar. It feels totally normal to walk in with my baby and with my mum and we have a really nice, fresh-tasting lunch which all feels a bit healthy, but we'll rectify that later. Mum asks if there is anything I need from Boots and I remember that I have been meaning to buy a razor since mine was taken off me when I arrived. I could practically plait my armpit hair. We head there and as soon as we step through the doors, I seem to transform into the Laura I know, perusing the aisles and chucking stuff into the basket. Apparently, I'm doing a shop akin to a pre-holiday shop and this is going to be way over £100.

As we get to the baby aisle, I walk past all the lovely bath products and ask Mum when she started using products with me and my brothers when we were babies. She obviously can't remember but doesn't see why we shouldn't be using them on Arthur. I haven't discussed this with Rhys, and I wonder if I should before I buy anything. While I'm thinking, Mum selects one and throws it in the basket, decision made. We get to the till where she finally pops in Maltesers and insists on paying. Now I'm into the swing, I wonder if there is anywhere else we can go. I spot a card shop and realise I need to get one to send to my twin brother. Every year, without fail, I'm so wrapped up in myself, I forget it's his birthday on the same day.

It's lovely to see Mum pushing the pram. The pram that she and George offered to buy us before Arthur was born, the pram that had so many hours invested in it, researching and test-driving to find The One. This one is lighter, but this one has a bigger basket. This one you can take on a plane as hand luggage but this one has big tyres so will be better in the park. Once we had narrowed it down, I ordered it from the local independent shop and waited for Mum to visit so we could collect it together. I realise that having a baby is much like Christmas Day. All the excitement is in the build-up and when it gets here, it's all a bit blah. Just me? Yup, thought so.

I decide I need a belt to go with my jeans. I don't like a pair of jeans without a belt. I could barely tell you what day it was when we were packing, let alone pick out a belt to go with the two pairs of jeans Mum packed for me. Oh, that reminds me, I must find that checked shirt when I get home.

We go into Oliver Bonas on the high street and find one but it's £30 and I'm on maternity leave and I'm not used to spending money, so I say I'll leave it. I have belts at home.

As we are walking home, we go past a fast-fashion shop and Mum suggests we have a look in there. I don't know the shop so the snob in me pops out and looks at her in disgust. 'Let's just give it a go,' she says, striding in confidently with the pram. I find the belt section and immediately smell them to check for cow. They're plastic, so they won't last for ages but, hey, they are £3 each. So, egged on by Mum, I get two. We walk away from the till having a giggle at ourselves (well, at me). Mums are always right.

On the way home, I take her to the good old café, the one where I know what I'm getting and have messaged her about many times. I order us carrot cake and cappuccinos, standard, and we get Arthur out of the pram so he can join in. I find myself taking hundreds of photos of Mum and him. She's in her element, she can't stop looking at him and laughing at everything he does. This is nice, this is what it should have been like from the beginning. I'm pleased she can have this moment with her grandson and, if I close my eyes for a second, we could be in a coffee shop in Cheltenham on a normal day having walked from a normal house and not from a mental hospital. I tell her Sue's back story as we walk home as I don't want her to put her foot in it. I can see her noting it down in her head.

When we get back, there is just enough time for Mum to assemble the cake in the kitchen and pop the Maltesers she got earlier around the top. Oh yes, and she gets out a slab of flapjack and a Victoria sponge I'm to give to Rhys when he next visits. And another large box of Maltesers, for me to share with my 'new friendies' and the staff apparently. The bag is finally empty.

I marvel at her. She just keeps going. She's always positive but having heard her do proper chat to Kim all those weeks ago, I realise that when it matters, she can cut through the happy-go-lucky exterior and have an opinion and make a decision. I get a flashback of what she must have been like in her working days, a proper young professional working efficiently at a million miles an hour. She totally deserves the slow pace of life she has now, and I make a mental note never to ask her 'what are we doing next?' when I next go to stay and have just finished breakfast.

As I come back from making Arthur's bottles, I can see Mum hugging Sue at the entrance to my room. I knew it.

Mum always likes to get to a train station about thirty minutes before the train actually leaves, making her already long journey home even longer. But that makes her happy, so I order the taxi and walk her outside. There are a lot of people outside the building and, unfortunately, she's walked into the path of the chap who only walks in straight lines and makes 90-degree turns, which has really thrown him off. I pull her out of his way as she starts to get more and more anxious that the taxi isn't there a minute before it's even due. She gives it another 30 seconds and asks me to call the company. How funny, I'm trying to chill her out stood outside a mental hospital that I live in, brilliant!

As I give her a long hug, I know that when I next see her, I'll be back home and operating at the same pace as her for the first time in about a year. How on earth she can be seventy I will never know. Seventy is no longer old in my world.

14TH SEPTEMBER

I've just had a Video Interactive Guidance (VIG) session with the psychologist. I'm not really sure what I made of it. It felt really forced to be watched and filmed playing with Arthur but apparently it was going to help my bond with him. I really am willing to give anything a go.

This is only the second session I have had with a therapist and it didn't really feel like a session as I was just playing with Arthur and the psychologist and I didn't actually speak. Apparently, we'll discuss the outcome next time we meet, whenever that might be. The first two weeks no one even mentioned seeing a psychologist, but by week three I was in and I realised how lucky I was. There is only one psychologist working for the ward at the moment, I think, and I don't think she's full time. I know some of the other girls haven't had any talking therapy as there simply isn't the capacity, but I guess I get to see her because I'm a 'simpler case'. I've not been ill like this before so I guess there is not so much to unpick. I don't know for sure but I know I'm very lucky.

The first session was very similar to that first meeting I had with Dr B, just bringing her totally up to speed with how my life had ended up being here, in the National Centre for Mental Health. I understand the next session will be to go through the outcomes of VIG and we'll arrange another session if and when we can after that.

I'm ready for Rhys arriving. I've showered, washed and dried my hair and put makeup on, including the new bits from

Mum. I have lipstick on. I look chubbier but I look nice, I know that. But I also feel like a fraud. If I'm well enough to do these things, I don't deserve this room and this care.

Rhys arrives on time and says I look good and that feels really nice. It really is like he has picked me up for a date from my parents' house. Rather than asking my dad if I can go, he has to ask the nurse in charge. I don't really want to see them like this as they will know I'm a fraud too. Maybe when I'm out, they will reallocate my bed?

As we walk out of the hospital with Arthur in his pram, I feel like we finally look like a little family unit who has this together. Rhys loves it when we go over the bumpy pavement and Arthur's cheeks jiggle. He aims for all the jiggly pavement bits and it's so nice to see the pleasure he gets from this silly little thing.

Arthur is asleep by the time we get to the restaurant, so it really does feel like a romantic moment. I order a mocktail and we chat. I'm talking at him; I'm losing my train of thought and going into all sorts of rabbit holes, but it doesn't matter. He smiles and listens, and I can tell by the look on his face that he knows his Beanie is coming back.

On cue, right after dinner, Arthur stirs so Rhys picks him up out of his pram. I look over at the two of them and I'm jealous. I want to be holding Arthur.

This is the very first time this has happened, and I register the enormity of this moment immediately. It makes me smile.

I keep asking Rhys if I can have him. I get the vibe that he likes hearing me say it. Arthur is three-and-a-half months old and this is the first time he has probably heard me ask to hold him.

We stupidly think we'll get a coffee in after dinner but predictably, just as they arrive, Arthur starts to grumble. I'm okay with that, it's about half an hour before his last bottle of the day, so he's just starting to let us know.

The nurses in the hospital are shocked how 'robotic' Arthur is with his feeding. Feeding on demand was one of my biggest moans to anyone who would listen. I couldn't make head nor tail of it, especially once we were bottle-feeding and bottles had a two-hour time limit on them. I'd want him to take all I had made or for him to want to feed again in the two-hour window so I didn't waste the milk. I told nursery nurse Anika this one time we were out walking and, rather than offering up something useless to me like 'Well, some days you eat more than others, don't you? And some days babies are more hungry than others', she said: 'Right, how old is he? Okay, he should be feeding every three hours or so, so just feed him every three hours or so'. And so, I did. That was the first time I had heard anyone 'maths' a baby and it was music to my ears. His first bottle was usually around 08:00, so everyone knew him as 'eight, eleven, two, five, eight'. He would often have a bottle in the night and his last one would usually come a bit early but, generally, in the day, he stuck to exactly this. And everybody who looked after him knew, if they messed up this rota for me…

We got home just before 20:00, gave him a quick bath together and Rhys gave him his last bottle before heading

asked me if I wanted her to do the feed, I thanked her very much and climbed back into bed.

Waking up thirty minutes later and really annoyed with myself, I try to put it behind me as I know Rhys will be coming soon.

He arrives bright and early and not looking too ropey – I am shocked! He stayed at one of the cricket boys' places last night as they had been out on Broad Street. God knows what time they got in, but he has managed to get to the hospital by 09:30, in a shirt and not smelling of booze, fags or puke. My expectations were low, so I was impressed.

He is super-enthusiastic, which quickly rubs off on me. We open some presents that people had left for me at the house and I pop his present – a canvas that he has made for me from the photos I have been sending him – proudly on the windowsill.

After thirty minutes, I can see he is flagging so I try to ramp up the enthusiasm and ask him what we are doing. 'Errr, well, I thought we could chill and then go for the lunch you've booked with your brother.'

Chill is all I ever do! I want to do something, something fun, within the rules of course. I know he wants to chill but much like any other day, today is especially all about me as it is my birthday. So, I drag him to what I hope will be a lovely little independent coffee shop, but all we can find is the Starbucks attached to the university. I have a disappointing hot milk with a hint of coffee and then we wander back to the town where we are meeting my brother.

As we are so early, Rhys suggests a drink. A totally normal thing to do but I've not had a drink for months. Actually, it is probably nearly a whole year. I don't know what to do or if it is allowed but then a 'fuck it' vibe washes over me and before I know it, I am ordering a Prosecco.

When we've finished, we walk up to the pub, and I feel well and truly like I am on a boat.

It is good to see Tom. It feels like I haven't seen him for years, but I guess the last time was when I'd randomly asked if he could bring envelopes and salad when he visited – the crazy days and only a short three months ago. He always makes an effort to see my twin brother and I on our birthday, he is a good big brother.

I have indigestion from the fizz quickly followed by a large glass of Pinot Noir. I don't really know anything about wines but an amazing old boss of mine in London always used to drink that when I travelled with him, so I'd follow suit. You never forget good bosses, do you? Whenever I peruse a wine list, I often think of him and smile inside at how great that role was and how lucky it was that a northern, engineering lass who usually speaks her mind managed to land such a brilliant role working for him against some stiff competition. She would never get that role nowadays.

Anyway, I am so blown up with indigestion, I can hardly manage any of my Sunday lunch, but I enjoy the wine and thinking back to Work Laura, Little Miss Confidence.

I go to get another round of drinks – water for me, we are going back to the hospital soon for Arthur's bath and I am very aware I need to be less wobbly. The bar is crowded and I notice that it is a pretty trendy gastro pub and that all the glam, good-looking girls are getting served and dumpy, mental me is getting overlooked. I sack off the round, go back to the table and tell the boys it is time to go back to the hospital.

In the daylight walking home, I feel guilty for having had a drink. I've had two. And the second one was large, so I've probably had about four. Jesus, the guys in the hospital were doing their best to make me better and I go and ruin it by getting pissed. As soon as I get back, I am pleased to see nurse James on shift and I ask if I can have a word. I go into the office and tell him that I may or may not have had a drink with lunch. He smiles, says he would expect nothing less, taps the side of his nose and walks out. Phew, I am not in trouble, but I suspect I won't get my usual dose of sleeping tablets tonight.

When I get back to my room, there is a card waiting on the bed for me that's been made using Arthur's footprint, and a heap of chocolates from my fellow crazies. Considering they are all going through their own rubbish, they are incredibly thoughtful.

17TH SEPTEMBER

At ward round, Dr B has suggested adding another kind of antidepressant to the Venlafaxine to give it a little boost. He asks if I'm okay with that. Of course I am, I'll do anything you say. So, we're going to add Mirtazapine to my daily haul. I'll take it at night instead of the sleeping tablet as apparently, at low doses, it has a sedating effect. I like the way he describes the two of them together as the Rolls-Royce of antidepressants. I feel very honoured to be on the RR of ADs and I cannot imagine what my bill must have got to by now. The only downside is that Mirtazapine can cause weight gain. Sigh.

'I think we should start talking about some home leave too,' says Dr B. The look on his face gives away the fact that he knows I've been expecting this.

'Okay, I know I've pretty much outstayed my welcome and I'll have to go at some point', I say defensively.

'You have absolutely not outstayed your welcome. You will be here for as long as you are poorly and need to be. There is no disputing that. We just think that now we have your sleep under control and I know this new drug is going to help you even more, and you have started your therapy, in the weeks coming we'll just start to think about taking some home leave.'

I don't really want to go home but I've known since my night out wearing makeup, it's been coming.

'Sorry, yes, of course. How will home leave work for me?' I ask.

Seeing the panicked look on my face, Dr B explains.

'Home leave will be a long process, Laura. We'll just start with a couple of hours, building up to a day. When the time is right, we can try some overnight stays at home.'

'Okay, I'm up for that', I reply, with the mantra from James in my head – *trust the process, Canty.*

The birthday cake Mum made me has been going down well. There is a new lady here who enjoys a slice for breakfast. She was admitted a few days ago, probably the day Mum came down, and she's still in her medical gown. Apparently, she came straight from the maternity ward up the road as she started showing signs of psychosis soon after the birth of her baby. She smells pretty bad now. The nurses have been trying to encourage her to go in the shower, but she doesn't have time, she's all over the place, up and down the corridor, stopping at every bedroom for a chat. She's accompanied 24/7 by an HCA, which is a bit of a relief as she really likes touching. The last time I saw her in the corridor, she stroked Arthur's cheek and told me it was good to see the rash had cleared up. She's the first lady I have seen with really quite extreme psychosis and it actually scares me a bit. It's random, happens to one in a thousand women apparently and there is no knowing why. I know this as I stopped to read one of the brochures she had taken out of the stand and started to organise down the length of the corridor.

18TH SEPTEMBER

The psychologist has just popped to my room to show me the photos she took during the VIG session the other day. I'm looking at Arthur and he's looking back at me while we're both on the play mat. Apparently, we'll discuss what I think this photo shows and some little clips of video she has in our session later this morning. I know she wants me to say I felt connected to him, but I didn't, I didn't feel anything. I rarely feel anything. I just keep thinking that my thighs look ginormous.

Our session mainly focuses on my values. I'm learning that values develop as you grow up, they are not things that you sit down and decide once you hit puberty. And until you start looking into behaviours, you probably won't be aware that you have these values.

We've homed in on the fact that one of mine is 'if you're not busy, you're not a worthwhile person'. We can't quite word it right, but we know what we mean, and it explains a lot. My whole life, I have always had to be busy. Even if I'm just at home, I want to clean or sort or tidy. From this value, a few rules seem to have appeared without me knowing about them. I can't watch TV or go to the cinema in the daytime. I can't work in a messy house, I have to make sure everything is tidy before I can go to bed or work from home. 'Chilling' is a waste of time. They go on.

Since I was little, I have operated like this and when I think about it, it's no wonder I've malfunctioned. Lots of friends take the micky that my brothers and I have never seen *Bambi* or any of the Disney films really. If we were sat watching the TV on a Saturday morning, we knew we were being naughty, and we were just waiting for Dad to come and drag us out to help him.

I don't see anything wrong with this. I like being busy, I like having a lot of things on. I work better under pressure and when I haven't got a lot on, I very quickly lose my motivation. When I'm tidying, I often start feeding the dog or loading the dishwasher or, or, or…I must walk round and around in circles putting things in the places they belong as I know that if I have to look at something not in its right place time and time again, it will really stress me out. So, it's easier to just tidy as I go.

This was fine when I lived on my own, but since living with a boy, I have OBVIOUSLY had to relax these rules a bit. I find it so hard to understand why Rhys watches TV in the day while trying to do a quote for work, I just can't understand how someone can concentrate like that.

These things are instilled from a young age and they can explain behaviour. It's really making me think about the things I say and do and how they will affect (adversely or not) my son.

I'm working with the psychologist to try to relax the 'always have to be busy' mantra. I'm trying to work on being in the moment, rather than looking for the next thing. This is where mindfulness comes in. I'm also trying to factor in chill time and learn to enjoy it rather than view it as a waste of time. I live with and love an Aussie and if there is one nationality we can learn chilling from it's those guys. That's probably why we work so well together. I make sure things get done and Rhys makes sure we get there in a way that's not going to lead to burnout.

Then the psychologist shows me the videos of Arthur and me. They're cute. They show him pretty much hanging on my every word. That's cool, I think, he likes me. I think I'm starting to like him too.

19TH SEPTEMBER

We're going swimming today. I don't know if it will actually happen or if anyone else will come. I suggested it in the weekly residents' meeting when they were asking if there were any activities we particularly wanted to do this week. It's a bit of a jump from going out for coffee but I was in a really positive mood in the meeting so I tried to think of the thing that would push me the most. And it's swimming. So many logistics involved and actually being in a swimming costume for the first time since giving birth, well, that's just terrifying.

When I was at home walking laps with Juliet and Edie, she was desperate for us to do something fun together that would take my mind off being anxious. As the weather was amazing, she suggested the lido a few times. Just hearing the word made me recoil. There was no way on earth that I would even contemplate it. Arthur didn't have trunks or swim nappies, I'd have to wear my maternity swimming costume, I'd have to pack a bag with everything in it, we'd have to get there and get them both changed and us changed and the list went on. I couldn't even picture the pool, there were so many questions about how to make it happen that I just wouldn't entertain it.

Today I've packed a bag. Arthur will be wearing a swim nappy given to me by my neighbour, who is coming too. He doesn't have swimming trunks but apparently that's okay. Cool. I have my cossie packed so I'm wearing everything I will change back into now. There is no chance, therefore, of forgetting a bra. I'm pretty sure I'm ready so I start to loiter in the corridor hoping to see the OT who has volunteered to take us, to ask if the trip is still on.

It is! They have packed their things and brought them to work. Bless them, I imagine this is their worst nightmare too, but they work for the NHS so of course they will go above and beyond to help their patients. Three of us want to go so we agree a time that will work for everyone. We're going to walk, setting off at 13:30 so we can get to the pool just before Arthur's 14:00 bottle. The plan is to feed him at the pool (I like the way a further challenge has been slipped in), which means we can get familiar with our surroundings. We'll then let the milk digest, have a splash and hopefully the babies will sleep on the way home. I love a plan! I have butterfly nerves in my tummy but I'm totally up for this.

I did it! We did it! As a crazy little team, we went, we conquered and now I'm over the moon!

Everything went according to the plan. There was a changing room for mums and babies and a pool that was at the perfect temperature, so Arthur didn't even register he was in the water. Arthur loved it. I didn't hate wearing my cossie. One of the mums who came but didn't swim took some photos and I don't look horrendous in them. I got us both changed and didn't drop any of the dry clothes onto the wet floor. The babies slept in their prams and I feel like I floated home on cloud nine. I'm pretty sure I didn't stop talking all the way back, I was just so proud of us and what we had achieved. I think I actually started to picture being on maternity leave at home – doing these kinds of things without overthinking them. I just need the actual feeling of enjoyment to come back and replace those butterflies.

I'm now actually pleased I didn't go to the lido all those months ago. I'm sure it would have been fine but the controlled way everything has happened today gives me the much-needed confidence that I could do it again. It's like I'm not the first mum ever to have taken a baby swimming before, who would have thought!

Actually, I just realised I didn't tell Rhys before we went. Maybe he wanted to take Arthur swimming for the first time. That hadn't crossed my mind once.

CHAPTER 8

DAY TRIPPING

22ND SEPTEMBER

The last time Rhys was here, he spent time with one of the OTs planning my first bit of leave home. I'm going home for two hours today. I'm not sure why, I'm not sure what I'm supposed to achieve in that two hours, but if I remember my sessions with the psychologist, I don't have to 'achieve' anything. I've been worried about this day for ages now. The day I have to start taking home leave. Some people take it every weekend if they can and they are local, and I don't know if it's a good thing. But yes, it had to happen, and I have to remember what I have learned and trust the process.

That being said, I simply can't operate without a plan. I have to know what I'll be doing with the time I'll be at home and the OT gets that, thank goodness. Rhys has agreed that all the building bits will be out of the house and that it will generally be clean and tidy. We are to take Alma for a walk, make a hot drink, spend time downstairs in the house and the garden and then it will be time to come back to the hospital.

I'm going home with Rachel, an OT, for this first visit and that makes me feel better. I also now have a plan and I know Rhys is ready for our arrival. I can't quite believe that we'll be going back to Cheltenham in a taxi when there is a train that goes from the hospital to Cheltenham but that's the way it's done.

The taxi picks us up at 09:00 and Arthur falls asleep pretty much as soon as we hit the motorway. I chat to Rachel a bit and I'm pretty chilled.

As we come off the motorway and I know exactly where I am, I can feel mild panic in my tummy but it's 'normal' levels of panic, panic that I can deal with.

We get closer and closer and it dawns on me that I have been away for a long time. As we pull into my road, my brain doesn't seem to be able to process everything. Rhys steps out of the front door onto a front drive that I don't recognise. There is now a paved front drive and a flower bed as opposed to the mud pit. I can't believe my eyes. Before I manage to get to Rhys for a hug, Alma runs over and, of course, pees on my feet. I'm pleased, because that's (quite literally) the warmest greeting you can get from a spaniel. She remembers me and she's excited to see me and I'm relieved. I bend down to try to pat her while her whole body squirms around, her tail wagging so much she can't stand still. Her ears are just as velvety as I remember and it's comforting to once again be stroking them. I then walk the short distance across the drive to have a sobby hug with Rhys. I realise that Rachel must think this is quite an extreme reaction to seeing him when he was only at the hospital a few days ago. So I explain to her about the drive.

I walk around and around it and spend time looking at all the flowers in the flower bed that's been created at the side of the drive. Apparently Ellie and her mum, Jo, are responsible for the flowers and Rhys has obviously worked tirelessly when he's had any spare time to lay the drive. I love him so much. He knew it upset me and he's sacrificed his precious chill and sleep time to do this for me. I imagine that sentence in the letter from the psychiatrist going over and over in his mind: 'Our house is the embarrassment of the street'. I feel my cheeks go hot. But oh, I could happily sit on this drive for two hours waiting for the taxi to pick us up.

We go inside and I slowly reacquaint myself with the kitchen and the living room while also feeling like I have to show Rachel around a house I barely remember. There is not a trace of building anywhere. Not even a pencil or a tape measure. Boy done good.

I open some post and then I'm keen to get out to the park with Alma. We do a couple of laps and I know Rachel is keen to let us talk but I want to include her so this whole thing doesn't seem odd, so I make her walk with us and we just chat. We stop for coffee at the little café in the park and it's just nice. It's nice and it's chilled. Girl done good.

Just before the taxi is due to turn up, I'm sad to admit to Rhys that I'm ready to go back to what has become my home, my institution. I want to get back to Room 7, the hustle and bustle of the hospital; I want to fill all the girls in on my new driveway.

Ellie pops in to say hi and I'm pleased as I can thank her in person for the flowers they have planted. Rachel has been sitting in the lounge to allow us all time in the kitchen. We're chatting away when Rachel pops her head in to say that the taxi guy has just called and the traffic is so bad out of Birmingham that they have not even left yet. I ask her what the next plan is. There isn't one, she obviously didn't realise this was going to happen and I can feel that slight panic start to bubble up. She says she's going to call her boss and ask what she should do. Okay, it's okay, they are going to make a plan and we will get back to the hospital tonight. It's okay, it's going to be okay.

As this is happening, Ellie and Rhys discuss the train. Of course, it's a five-minute drive to the train and then we can just walk at the other end, the train station is close to the hospital. And we have the car seat as that's how we brought Arthur in the taxi, so Rhys can drop us at the station, perfect. Well, kind of perfect. I actually do have to do it now.

When Rachel comes into the room, Rhys explains the new plan to her. Unfortunately, this is the exact opposite of what her boss has advised – to just sit tight until the taxi arrives, in hopefully two hours' time. I don't want to do that; I have just got my head around getting the train for the first time with a baby and I want to get back to the hospital for Arthur's next feed and his bedtime routine. We ask her to call her boss back and, after a lot of persuading (apparently it's quite a process to recover the costs of the train ticket), her boss agrees. I'm pleased and I'm so relieved I'm with Rachel.

As we're merrily chugging our way back to Birmingham, train on time, seats sourced, we both get a whiff of dirty nappy. It goes through my head to just leave it until we get back to the safety of the changing table in Room 7, but we have only been going about ten minutes. I know I have to change it. The train is rammed. I can't get to the toilet so, bravely, I ask the people sat opposite if they mind me changing my baby on the seats. They don't seem enthusiastic about it, but they say they don't mind so I get on with it.

I spend the rest of the journey and the rest of the day so proud of myself that I have not only dealt with uncertainty, but I have changed a nappy in non-ideal circumstances. I was calm on the outside but, more importantly, I was calm on the inside too.

24TH SEPTEMBER

Dr B is away this week but I still see the entourage, just with a different person at the helm. We discuss the home leave and even though it's gone well, I stress that I was excited to come 'home'. And that home to me was still the hospital. When I think of Cheltenham as home, it makes the sick bubble rise in my throat and my mind turns to black again.

They all discuss going to the maximum dose of Venlafaxine and doubling the Mirtazapine. I remember that this was only sedating at low doses, so I ask about that. The consultant reassures me that I started on such a low dose that the next dose up should still have the sedating effect. I don't want to ask if they think Dr B would have done the same as I don't want it to sound like I don't trust them, so I go with it. I'm sure he would have done, and I can ask him next week.

25TH SEPTEMBER

It was all going so well and then I puked. As I was about to give Arthur his bath, a wave of sickness suddenly came over me. Thank goodness one of the HCAs was walking past the bathroom at the time. I swear Arthur got some air between me and her as I pretty much threw him over and went to stick my head down the toilet. How weird. I felt totally fine before.

The staff got me some water and I sat on my bed while someone else bathed Arthur and put him to bed. I'm so lucky to be here. I'd got to the point where I felt okay and not like I was going to throw up again when a nurse came in to see me in a plastic apron. She explained that because I had thrown up, I had to be in isolation for 72 hours. That's one, two, three whole days! I've only been sick once and now I seem fine. But rules are rules and I'm not at guide camp, I'm in a hospital.

So that was it, now there is a metal table outside with a poo chart on. I have to record every poo and allocate it a shape based on the photos. If anyone cares to look, they can see how often I've been to the loo and whether I consider that trip to be 'separate hard lumps, like nuts' or 'like a sausage or snake, smooth and soft'. There are seven categories of poo apparently, seven. The only other things on my table are a box of gloves, a bag of plastic aprons and a jug of water that someone has to fill up for me as it won't fit under my tap.

Apparently, Arthur can still go to crèche even though I'm not allowed out and I'll still be able to have my psychology appointment in my room with the psychologist in the plastic get-up. Meals are going to be brought to me and I basically just have to be okay in this room for the next 72 hours unless I puke again, and the time will be extended.

I've been pretty down about this, but Rhys has just texted to say he's going to get Alma back for good and I'm happy about that. I'm pretty sure he'll be spooning her as I write this.

27TH SEPTEMBER

I spend most of the day in bed. I think this is the first time I have thought about my physical health, apart from realising I'm putting on weight of course. I had just got into the stride of going for runs a couple of times a week and to the gym, on a Wednesday between 14:00 and 15:00. That's the only time our ward is allowed to go to the gym as it is shared between all wards and is also used by outpatients. The gym is part of the physio department, which is located in the basement. On my first visit, I noticed there were more Zimmer frames outside the gym than equipment inside it.

One of the personal trainers (PTs) is a lady who I really like. She's a mum so she 'gets it'. She had been hospitalised for most of her pregnancy as she had such severe morning sickness. I'm not sure how she came out of that with a smile on her face, but she did and she also appreciates the need to feel fit once you have 'got your body back'. She is always so enthusiastic and would do anything she could to ensure you got your weekly visit. She comes to teach us Tai Chi on the ward every Tuesday morning, after which she tries to get people enthusiastic about training the next day. A thankless task on a ward full of depressed people who just want to stay in bed, but every week she is full of beans and eager to get as many people to the basement as possible.

Needless to say, it is usually only me. I once persuaded a fellow patient down. She said she loved it straight after the session and would definitely do it again next week...

The other PT could not be more opposite. He is a slightly dumpy bloke who doesn't seem to be bothered. He spends most of my sessions checking himself out in the mirror and throwing a pen in the air and sometimes catching it. He really thinks he is God's gift and let's face it, in a mental hospital he probably is. One session, he asked me to stop after six minutes of cycling, he then reminded me that I'd done five minutes the week before, so I've made progress, real progress. *Well, technically*...I opened my mouth to counter this but realised I could not be bothered, it wouldn't be worth it. I'm sure he'll go home happy with himself and that's cool. Eventually, he just left me to it, which I think suited both of us.

28TH SEPTEMBER

After spending two and a half days in isolation, the results have come back and I don't have anything infectious, so I'm allowed out. I'm halfway between being mad that I have been stuck in here bored, and not really caring. I rationalise it by telling myself it's only been a couple of days and there is not much to do anyway.

I've also completed at least five giant dot-to-dots from the book my uni pal Amy brought me all those weeks ago. I don't think I have done any puzzle-type activities for about thirty years, but I really enjoyed them. Now that is a turn-up for the books and something I might have to add to my little tool kit when I'm on the outside.

Maybe the chilled side of me is finally crawling out.

Another bonus of being out and free from infection is that I get to go to my session with the psychologist in her room and with her not dressed in plastic. I know how lucky I am to have access to these sessions as there are so few slots and I'm keen to make the most of them.

In last week's session, we had started exploring my values after talking a lot about my need to always be busy, to be doing things, to be productive, to be achieving. I regularly find that just as we think we are getting to something, the hour is up, so I'm looking forward to picking up where we left off. Hopefully today we'll get to some conclusions and something I can actually use in my life from this point.

29TH SEPTEMBER

Today, I'm going home for the whole day. There are a couple of objectives to my trip. The first is to go into my bedroom and, more importantly, the ensuite. Objective number two is to try to make the house feel more like a home. When the OT and I spoke about this, we decided to aim to get some pictures up on the walls and get some candles. Basically we are to *hygge* the s*it out of it! Rhys is going to love it.

'*Hygge*' is a term that has only recently been introduced to me. A friend of a friend has sent me a couple of parcels and they have pretty much blown me away. The parcel process in here is pretty exciting on its own. The ward receptionist comes to tell you you have something to pick up, so you have to go to the main reception with a nurse and that's a fun activity in itself. You might get to see some of the other patients from the other wards – who wouldn't be curious about that? Or maybe it's just that I'm nosey. I don't care, I have a parcel! Then the anticipation of walking back to the ward, asking the nurses for scissors, being supervised to use them and then marvelling at the contents.

The first package she sent me had a little bottle of frankincense in. I didn't know what it was for but as I read the little card, I started to well up with a big smile on my face. It was from Rosie, one of Bec's friends who had thought of me. How nice is that? Not only had she thought of me, she'd thought about me enough to think of what I might want, go out and get it, look up the hospital address, go to the post office in her lunch hour (which is always a ball ache), line up and send it.

It was remarkable. Not only that I had received a little something, but that it was from someone I really didn't know that well, apart from through Bec when I'd ask after her and when we'd see each other at a social event. I resolved to make sure I go out for coffee or wine with Rosie when I'm out and thank her in person. I think that's when she'll transition from Rosie, 'friend of a friend', to 'my friend Rosie'. That will be nice.

Shortly after that, I received another parcel from her. It was a book called *A Year of Living Danishly*. It's a non-fiction book about a journalist who moved to Denmark when her husband got a transfer with work. She made it her mission while there to understand why Denmark is the happiest country in the world. She found that it was down to a number of things, but one of them was this thing called *hygge* – basically, making a fabulous environment for yourself and your family in your home. So the Danes, more than any other country, spend lots of money on nice lamps, cushions, candles, flowers and so on. I love all these things, and this has made me more determined to get the lounge and our bedroom finished when I'm out. Great shout, Rosie!

***

The taxi picks Arthur and I up at 09:00 and we are on our own this time. It is nice to pull up on that drive again and it is nice to know that one of our objectives is to go shopping.

In true me-style, we only spend about ten minutes at home before walking into town. We end up stopping for a sit-down lunch and then going on to buy photo frames, candles and some stems of eucalyptus and pussy willow. By the time we get home and have finished *hygge*-ing the living room, we only have about ten minutes to complete objective number one before the taxi arrives to take us back.

I walk upstairs to the landing and then stop and look up the next set of stairs to the loft where our bedroom is. As I go up them, I hear the familiar squeak of the third step. I'd forgotten about that until now. I open the door to the bedroom and stand there, looking around every bit of it. It smells a little, not unpleasant but not something I recognise straight away. Maybe fibreglass? Of course, it would be Rhys's work trousers in the wardrobe.

I walk slowly into the ensuite. It's grey. Two different kinds of tiles but both grey. The day we picked these tiles we were not having a very functional day. I was heavily pregnant and we had to pick the tiles that day as tiling was the next job on Rhys's list. We were normally good at making house decisions and making them quickly (we'd had a lot of practice) but this particular day we were just not getting on, the team wasn't working. So, we'd ended up with grey and a lot of it.

There is still a little box of panty liners near the loo which Rhys obviously has not thought to move. The box has a thin layer of dust over the top like it has always been there. I look at the sink and see the solitary toothbrush in its holder. That makes me sad. Poor Rhys, every night going to bed alone, not knowing when the home he had made would be full of laughter again.

The window is opposite the sink; I turn my head and there it is, closed and small. *The hours I have spent staring at you and out of you, little window.* I feel a lump in my throat and a slight feeling of disbelief. How could I have contemplated that? What a silly, silly girl. I make myself look at it for what seems like hours. The lump slowly disappears, to leave a feeling of relief and total gratefulness. I am grateful that I am being saved. Saved from the thoughts I used to have, those nasty, vivid, persistent, evil thoughts.

I've done it, I've completed the objectives the hospital asked and I am pleased. It is time to close the door, knowing I will be back and it will be okay. That was in the past, it is time to move forward and it is time to make a change to that bathroom.

The next time I manage to save up, that bathroom is getting a new lease of life, a fresh, non-grey start.

Again, it's a relief when the taxi turns up and I'm pleased to be going back to the safety of the hospital. I'm worried that this will never change. Maybe I could live in the hospital? I know how things work by now. I could be the person who meets new patients at the main reception and then helps them settle in. I'm sure the NHS would have some funding for that. That sounds like a realistic thought, Laura.

I'm shattered in the taxi; I want to sleep but Arthur is still awake, so I try to keep him entertained by pointing at random things out of the window. I'm a bit mad with myself for doing so much today. I feel like I can, so I do, but driving back to the hospital brings it home. I'm an inpatient, I'm in recovery, I'm on a massive dose of tablets and I just need to try to remember everything we have talked about in psychology and learn to chill.

Just when I think the staff couldn't get any better, I hear when I get back that the night shift is going to hold a pamper party for us. A couple of the girls who have been here a while and are able to go out unescorted were given some petty cash and told to go and get some clay face packs and snacks.

At 20:00 when they come on shift, the team sets up the lounge as best they can. They have a foot spa going with bubbles in, and there is enough chocolate and cake to sink a ship. Once we all have on our 90p charcoal facemasks from Poundland, we take it in turns to use the foot spa and get a little shoulder massage. All of this while someone else makes proper hot chocolate with milk and marshmallows. I feel like this should be the other way around, that we should be treating the night staff before they run around all night sorting out all sorts of random stuff and, let's face it, perhaps even saving a life. What incredible people.

30TH SEPTEMBER

Today was another day trip home. This time, I'm to add friends into the mix. Rhys has invited Bec and Kate over for Sunday lunch with their son, Jude, who I can't believe is now two.

Rhys is a good cook, another 'good' box ticked in a potential husband, I know.

It was a really lovely day. The roast potatoes were on point, the bottle of wine tasted amazing and things reached fever pitch when we thought that Jude was going to crawl through the dog flap. But I'm still a bit annoyed with myself for wanting to come back to hospital. It was actually the perfect day. I enjoyed seeing Bec, Kate and Jude all at the same time. I enjoyed showing them what we had done the weekend before with the photos.

When our pals had gone home, Rhys and I sat in our newly *hygge*-ed living room, finishing our drinks and discussing the sofas we'd like to have in there when we could afford them. I realised there and then that money wasn't on my worry list any more. And in fact, I couldn't remember the last time I'd run through my worry list. I wasn't curious how the one-way system in town worked, I figured I'd just deal with it when I had to. It didn't matter RIGHT NOW that Rhys's name wasn't on all of the bills, we'd work through them when I was out. I had started having rational thoughts. Not worrying about things I had no control over and making plans to resolve things that didn't need resolving. Wow, I'm definitely getting better,

I know that now. How had a worry list been an actual thing? How could I have spent so much time worrying about the flipping one-way system? The drugs were working, the therapy was working, the hospital was working.

As I went to put my glass back on the coffee table, I noticed a small box on the shelf underneath it. Without picking it up, I squinted at the words on it – Sertraline. I knew I had tried out and was currently taking a lot of drugs, but I knew Sertraline, one of the most commonly prescribed antidepressants, was not one of them. I looked at Rhys and he knew what I had found. Ugh, had I broken him too?

'Are these yours?' I asked.

'Damn it, yes, you were not meant to see them.'

'Have you been to the doctor?' What a stupid question, of course he's been to the doctor.

'Look, I'm fine,' he insisted, but before we got to discuss it further, the taxi beeped and it was time to leave.

I strapped the car seat into the taxi and Arthur into the car seat and we waved Rhys and Alma goodbye. I was pleased to be able to report on my rational thoughts to the staff and pals in the hospital. I hoped Rhys would enjoy the rest of his evening. We'd had a nice day, nice food and good company so I hoped he'd now watch some rubbish TV with Alma and have a good night's sleep.

On the drive back, I processed what I'd found. Initially I was shocked and upset. I couldn't believe that I'd brought the dark cloud over Rhys as well. The more I thought about it, though, the prouder I was of him. He'd had some time and some space away from me and my depressed whirlwind and he'd thought about himself. Not only had he thought about himself, but he'd realised he didn't feel right and it had gone on too long. He'd actually picked up the phone, spoken to a doctor's secretary and asked to make an appointment. That is pretty amazing going for any man, let alone a man who doesn't like to talk about his feelings. Yes, I was proud and I knew we would work together to recover ourselves back to full strength.

1ST OCTOBER

I was super-pleased to see Dr B back. He's been at a conference; it turns out he really is the man in this field. I knew I was lucky to be here. He indeed confirms he's pleased his colleagues made the changes they did last week and we'll leave everything the same for this week. That's cool, I'm pleased with that. I still feel a little dizzy but it's definitely better than it was, definitely.

As the weather is better this afternoon, all of us have congregated in the little courtyard to feel some sun on our faces. Dark Glasses wanders out in her jeans and huffs and puffs, remarking how hot it is and disappearing again. Shortly afterwards, she comes back in a tiny pair of shorts, preaching to us that we all must get changed as it's such a lovely day. As no one moves, she disappears again and comes back with a sarong which she lays out on the concrete and looks at me as if to say 'in for a penny, in for a pound'. She pulls her T-shirt over her head so she can sunbathe in her bra, then lays down on the sarong.

I'm not sure if this has ever happened at The Barberry before, but it sure as hell is happening now and Dark Glasses is loving it while the rest of us just chuckle away. She gives it about three minutes, decides it isn't as hot as she thought, so she disappears off to perform her third outfit change of the day – love her.

3RD OCTOBER

Last night, there was definitely some funny stuff going on. When I was making breakfast, I noticed through the window that there were lots of sanitary towels in the garden.

Later on, at lunch, I found out that Psychosis Girl had got into a few of the bedrooms and had been throwing them at people in their sleep last night. I didn't quite understand how she had managed to get past the HCAs to be able to do this, but okay. They went on to tell me that once she was caught for the second time, she had a tantrum and started throwing them around outside and tidying up had just been futile.

I was told all this while I watched the lady in question pour salt and pepper into her drink. I didn't really know what I should do. Just as she'd managed to take a sip, I alerted an HCA and she had it taken off her. I asked her what it was like. Good, apparently, it was really bland before.

4TH OCTOBER

The nurses have told me that Arthur's second set of injections are at 10:45 this morning at the local surgery. They asked me if I wanted someone to come with me and it didn't take me long to think. I knew I had to test myself. 'No, thank you, I'll be fine', I hear myself replying.

I get there early, obviously, and stand in the queue at the front desk to check in. As I look around, I notice the waiting room is full and a couple of elderly women smile at me. At the front of the queue, I confidently give both of our names. The lady looks at the computer and says she can't see us, am I sure that I have the right day? Oh God. I don't really feel the panic like I used to, but I know this isn't good as the plan was to have the jabs, feed robot Arthur at 11:00 and then he would sleep it off on the walk home. She must see my panicked face as she asks me when I booked. This means I'm allowed to tell her my sob story that I'm in The Barberry and it's too far to take him to his home surgery in Cheltenham and the admin lady told me he was registered here and he had his other jabs here and…She smiles at me and asks if I can come back in thirty minutes; she will find a nurse to do them then. I am welcome to sit in the waiting room to save me going back to the hospital if I like.

'Okay, that's fine, thank you very much for fitting me in.' I turn around and, without really thinking, I am striding to my favourite coffee shop. I am only going to go and bloody well do the impossible. My plan is to go to the café, find a table, order my coffee and then feed Arthur right there, in a café. On my own! I can feel the adrenaline shot that has just been released as I give myself an internal pep talk.

I'm relieved the café is pretty quiet and I find a seat that doesn't involve too much disruption with the pram and doesn't take up too much space. I park, pick my purse out of the change bag (which I packed myself with no dramas) and then pick Art out of the pram. We saunter, casually, to the counter and order a skinny cappuccino please, no, no cake. And would I like a babycino for the little one? No thanks, he's brought his own. I am having chat with a stranger, including MY SON and we are all smiling.

Before sitting down, I get Arthur's bottle out of the bag and simply sit down and give it to him. When my coffee arrives, I expertly locate the sugar, put half a packet in, give it a stir and lick the chocolate off the spoon. As I take a sip of coffee, I even have a little look around. Is anyone watching me? I want people to be watching me, proof that I am doing it.

When Arthur's finished, I pop him on my shoulder for a little burp and pray to the vomit gods that he doesn't puke down my back. He doesn't. I then casually have my last sip, pop him back in the pram and wheel off in the direction of the surgery.

I've only been gone about 16 minutes, so we walk up and down the high street for a while and then go in. The lady at the desk is the same one, thank goodness. She smiles at me and mouths for me to take a seat.

There you are, Canty, you can do it. Brilliant. Now we just need to get those jabs in before he falls asleep and we have mission complete. Another 45 minutes go by and I realise I should probably call the hospital to tell them we're okay. They are relieved, they were going to give me another ten minutes and then call. They tell me that they are sorry about the mix-up and that they will investigate. I tell them not to, I don't want any blame to be assigned as actually it's helped me out. I tell them about my little coffee trip, and they seem so proud of me. They are the best.

By the time the nurse calls us through, Arthur has woken from his nap and it couldn't have worked out better. Arthur screams a little on the way back but who wouldn't? He's just been injected without knowing it was coming, poor little boy. I call the hospital back to ask if they will save me some lunch. They laugh, of course they will.

I give myself permission to sleep for the rest of the day if I want to. I'm determined to learn from the psychology I'm having. I'm to listen to what my body needs. If it needs sleep and I give it that, then that's productive. End of.

I smashed that!

5TH OCTOBER

Ward round morning and it goes well. We confirm I'm going to go home overnight tonight but that if I need to call, I must. If it gets to the evening and I get panicky, I can come back apparently. I don't want that to happen, I want to succeed, I want to do it. I want to get better.

***

Going home for a night is a bit different from going home for the day or just a few hours. I really have to concentrate on what I'm packing. I can't remember what I have at home, so I pack all the toiletries from the top of the sanitary bin into a bag and pop that in my case with two changes of underwear and a change of top. There must be stuff at home I can wear if I need to. I pack my makeup and feel somewhat guilty to be taking the communal hairdryer home. I'm the girl on the block to talk to if you want dry hair. Such a bad ass.

I go from packing straight to my session with the psychologist. I do like these sessions and I know they are helping but I'm so used to having a meeting with an agenda and a structure that it seems so odd just to go into these sessions and just talk about whatever I want to (or that's how they feel).

We discuss how I feel about going home and some coping mechanisms I have learned. I will remember to do my meditation or deep breathing if I feel I need to. I also need to remember to go against my deep-rooted value of 'you have to be busy to be achieving'. It's okay if I want to sit and chill or read or watch TV in the middle of the day. All of these things are okay; I just need to listen to my body and let the thoughts of what I should be doing go through my head and wave them off.

I know this will all be harder in practice but having this session means everything is front and centre of my mind just before I leave.

While I've been in the session, Philippa, my friend from school, has arrived and is waiting for me on the sofa in the corridor. It's so nice to see her. We haven't seen each other since I was home for Christmas but when she knew I was in hospital, she asked if she could come and it was, of course, a no brainer. I take her to the old faithful café for lunch and we talk about all sorts. It's funny, there are some friends you don't see for ages but when you finally meet up, you just pick up where you left off. She has a son too, but we don't do a load of baby chat and it's a refreshing change. It feels a bit like we're at school, talking about everyone on the ward and giggling away at things we both noticed but wouldn't tell anyone else. When we get back to the ward, she helps me to pack my things into the taxi and I wave her off. I still can't believe she came all this way but she did, and I appreciated it so I tell my brain to stop chitter-chattering that I should feel guilty.

We get home at about 16:30 and it's cool. I am cool. It feels okay to unpack and it feels really nice to have dinner at home, bath Arthur in the big bath and pop him to bed in his little cot that he's pretty much grown out of.

When we get into bed, it does feel a bit weird: (a) we have not gone to bed at the same time for I don't know how long, possibly before I was pregnant, (b) I have had a bed to myself for the last two months, and (c) I'm taking a tablet that I know will help me sleep but that's okay as, everything crossed, Arthur now sleeps through the night so there's no risk of half-awake trips down the stairs.

The last time my head was hitting this pillow, it was a very different head. But it now seems like the storm has calmed up there and it will actually allow my body to rest. The worry list has gone, or at least been put into perspective. There is no danger that Rhys will come into the room with Arthur in a few hours and disturb me, they are here beside me.

The bed sheets smell so clean and fresh and there is no plastic sheet rustling underneath me. I can't get over it, this is 180 degrees different from when I was last here. Sleep well, Canty, come on, sleep well.

6TH OCTOBER

I slept, I slept, I SLEPT!!! And Rhys has just got up with Arthur, who slept too! I'm having my first, non-guilty lie in. Rhys is downstairs with Arthur, giving him his first morning milk at home for a very long time. He's not with a nurse who has a million and one other things to do. He's with his daddy.

I'm in my bed, loving the clean sheets and the fact I'm in my house. I treat myself and lie like a starfish. I've been in a single bed for nearly two months.

I want to see the two of them together, so I get up, pop my dressing gown on and go downstairs to find them lying on the sofa together. Rhys looks so happy, I'm so relieved we have got to this stage. I couldn't ever imagine being in this house and feeling in any way calm and like I could cope, it's almost like a dream.

We both get ready to go for brunch with Bec, Kate and Jude as it was Becca's birthday yesterday. Who would have thought I'd be celebrating it, at home, in Cheltenham? Rhys gives Arthur his 11:00 milk and I notice the smile he had on this morning hasn't faded. He always found this easy, nothing has changed. He feeds him while sipping coffee and chatting, as he has always done, with complete ease. I've now proved to myself that I can do this without anything going wrong or anyone dying. It's just a shame it's taken me all this time to get to this stage.

I let these thoughts bubble through my head but manage to turn them quickly into what the rest of maternity leave holds. All the normal things we can do now and all the new experiences I can give Arthur in his home town.

After brunch, we take Alma over to the park and throw the ball for her. Arthur happily sleeps in his pram and all is good with the world. I think I'm enjoying it but, again, I can't feel any tingles or anything inside. I know I'm overthinking about my feelings and it's annoying me.

When Alma is panting so hard she can't keep her tongue in her head any longer, we figure it's time to go home. And I'm okay with that. I'm actually quite happy with that. We'll go back to the home that we have built, and it will be nice. And it is. We don't do anything 'productive' for the rest of the day and that is just fine.

Arthur hates his bath tonight, but we did it together in our home and we'll make him like it in time, I'm sure. I'm sure he'll be bribed with some good bath toys and my head is already racing ahead to being able to shop for him, to treat him just because I want to, and because I can. The prospect of walking to town is no longer a scary one. Rhys gives him his last bottle before bed and we have a couple of hours just lounging on each other, watching rubbish Saturday-night TV. I like this, I'm liking this.

Tomorrow, I know we are going back to Birmingham and, for the first time, I'm relieved that I don't really want to. Rhys is driving us as we are meeting up with my twin brother and his family for Sunday lunch so the cousins, who were born three weeks apart, can meet for the first time.

7TH OCTOBER

I slept like a log again. I think I actually squealed with excitement about it this morning. When Arthur woke, there was a bit of an 'Oh, I'll have to get up from my nice bed and I could do without that' but nothing like before. No chanting of 'this is hell', no running through the worry list, no rituals with lavender in the middle of the night. Yes, I'm still taking the sedating antidepressant pills before bed, but they can't knock me out for the whole night, my body must be allowing me to do some of it all on its own. Anyway, enough of this, I need to get everything packed up so we can head back, hopefully for the last week. I need to keep trusting the process right until the very end.

I'm back in Room 7 and we've just been for lunch with my twin brother and sister-in-law and I'm not sure how I feel. I have never seen my brother look so tired or stressed. It's the first time we have seen them since they have had their baby. They came to visit me in Gloucester Hospital the day after I had Arthur as they happened to be in the area for the weekend. It was so lovely to see them then and so brave, I thought. Claire must have been about eight months pregnant then, so I was impressed that she'd been for a weekend away and that she'd been to visit someone recovering from a caesarean section with her baby in an incubator. It's one thing watching it on *One Born Every Minute*, but a different thing seeing your sister-in-law in pain in real life. Kudos to her.

This morning, I dressed Arthur in an adorable pair of pale blue dungarees, edged in white with a rainbow across the pocket. They are from a pal I waitressed with in Hull a million years ago. I love that my friends have been so generous with clothes. I remember most of these outfits on their children and to see them having a new life on Arthur is just great. And they all have great taste (or have avoided passing on the rough pieces) so that works for me!

We met my brother at the pub. It was all a bit stressful, trying to get the buggies down the steps and find somewhere to store them, but once that drama was over, we relaxed and ordered some drinks. Well, I was definitely relaxed, it turns out I was the only one who ordered wine, oops. Look at me pretending I'm not a patient. We exchanged birthday presents and got loads of photos of the cousins together. I'm not sure we talked at all about the hospital, we did talk a lot about babies though and how much life had changed.

I felt sorry for Claire – she had to eat her dinner in a matter of moments so she could get back to feeding. Sam also seemed sorry for her, of course he would be. I know what it was like to feel that tired and that attached but it's a distant memory now. I cannot imagine what it feels like to breastfeed on demand. I definitely would not be in the place I am now if I had not given that up.

It makes me think how little I have been in touch with them since they have become parents and I feel guilty about that. I wanted us to have a nice time together today and I felt like we did and I hope they felt the same way too. Nothing about having a baby is easy, especially when you have had to drive such a long way and have such a hungry baby. I'm pleased the cousins have finally met and all those happy thoughts of them on their bikes together now seem like they might become a reality. I'm really relieved about that. Really, very, incredibly relieved. I've had a glass of wine.

I gave them both a massive hug goodbye and hope that I'll see them soon. As we walked away, I thought how different every baby is. Our son seems to have been okay with the transition to bottle-feeding. Apart from working out the volumes and us wearing the formula more times than it stayed in his tummy, it had gone relatively smoothly. He'd also got into a routine, which I totally credit the hospital for. I'm lucky, I seem to have a model child, it's just me that had an epic fail.

I guess everyone's maternity leave takes a different flavour and I think that's how I'm going to have to make peace with being in here. It seems to be a trade-off with babies and something that goes well for one person doesn't go so well for another and vice versa. We all know that comparing ourselves isn't helpful in any situation and so comparing myself as a mother to anyone else I see on social media, in magazines or on billboards is something I know I cannot do and cannot let contribute to another downfall.

I didn't like saying bye to Rhys today. This is a definite change, it used to not bother me. It's been really good to spend the weekend with him. I think he's sad to say bye to me too. We talk on the phone on his drive home to try to keep him awake. He sends me photos of Alma when he gets home and takes her to the park, and I send him photos of us. It won't be long until we are all back together again, I'm convinced of it.

8TH OCTOBER

I'm so pleased I'll be able to tell Dr B good things at ward round today. I can't believe it actually appears to be working. For most of my visits home, I've been ready to come back to the hospital, so I'm hoping that the feeling of wanting to stay at home this weekend wasn't a one-off. He was pretty right, wasn't he? Keep going, do what we say, and you will get better. I don't know how you define 'getting better', but not wanting to kill myself so I don't have to carry on living life with a baby is pretty good for me.

I guess 'better' means feeling like I used to, pre-Arthur, but if I'm honest I can't really remember what that feels like. And because I'm now thinking of my feelings all the time, maybe I'm overanalysing it. Before, if I felt a bit blue, I'd just do what felt right. I'd go and watch the TV, or go for a run or whatever, I wouldn't have a dialogue with myself about how I feel and what the right cause of action therefore is. Will I always do this now? Constantly be checking in with myself. Is that a bad thing? And what about the drugs I leave here on? Do I just keep taking them? Is it them that's truly making me tired and hungry? How do I function back in my 'normal' life while at the same time being tired and hungry?

And I don't want to feel just 'blah' for the rest of my life, I want to actually feel something inside. I want to have that feeling of being so overexcited about something that I could pop. But if I have to trade that for not feeling so bad that I contemplate something happening to my precious son, I'd take the pills every day of the week.

This is going to be a long meeting.

Everyone in the meeting agrees that it's time I extend my periods of home leave from the hospital after the success of my weekend away. We have decided that I'll have my planned therapies this week – psychology, physiotherapy, massage and acupuncture – and this time next week, we'll see if I'm ready to take the plunge and have a trial two weeks at home. It sounds like a pretty big ask but it's a good way to see if I can operate at home, doing my life.

It seems a long time ago when I was questioning why I wasn't getting intense therapies from the moment I walked through the door to now. But I now know that the most important thing was sleep. Sleep is the best healer. As long as I could get some sleep and become less of a zombie, the 'proper' treatment plan could be put in place to get me back to me.

The psychology sessions have focused on my values and my unhelpful or intrusive thoughts, using a combination of Cognitive Behavioural Therapy (CBT) and Compassion-Focused Therapy (CFT). Physiotherapy was then added to my treatment plan to deal with my knee pains. If I was to maintain a healthy lifestyle when I left hospital, my knees needed to be a part of that. Running is a great way of maintaining good mental health so as long as I could do it with no pain, that would be excellent. So, the physiotherapist helped with that and also introduced me to acupuncture. She'd used some needles in my knee and while they were there, she'd popped one in my forehead to help me relax and get a good night's sleep.

These sessions with the physio in the basement of the hospital had helped in establishing some 'me time' as I started to use the acupuncture to encourage natural sleep and allow me less dependency on the tablets.

Finally, massage was the best therapy of all. I had always enjoyed a pamper so to know we had this option open to us was wonderful. Again, this helped with breaking down the fact that I had to be with Arthur all the time and it was about getting a balance between being a mum and looking after mum. This also obviously helped to encourage natural sleep. What a lucky bug I was, having all this on the doorstep of Room 7, all available to help put me back together again and back into my life, physically and mentally well.

As I walk down the corridor to go and get dinner, I see Dark Glasses with her partner (so that's the guy who had the plant pot hit him on the head), her son who I have not seen before and the elusive baby in her pushchair. I barely recognise her. She's wearing knee-high boots, has makeup on and her hair is straightened. I guess that ward round for her has gone well and she's being discharged.

I really can't believe the change in her. I'm happy for her and wish her a cheerful 'good luck'. She looks straight through me as though she doesn't have a clue who I am. I don't know if this is because she's leaving and doesn't want to acknowledge anything or anyone to do with the hospital? Or is it because she's still not well and now she's playing a different character? One who doesn't know me? I have no idea what her diagnosis was, but maybe she's been living as someone else in here?

14TH OCTOBER

Holly and Chris are coming today. I've told them they really don't have to, but they are up this way visiting her parents so will call in on their way back to London. I want to see them but I'm feeling really guilty about being here and taking one of the precious beds. I'm sure they will see a normal, pre-baby Laura, and I'll seem like a drama queen, allowing myself to go to hospital when there is nothing wrong with me. I have a word with myself and remember the texts Kim sent me as she was referring me – I would not be referring you if you were not poorly enough to need to be there. Full stop.

They come to my room and it's so good to see them. It feels very odd to be here now and see how different I am from the new mums being admitted. We close the door and we're in a little bubble talking about how it's been going in here for me and life in the outside world for them. The last time I saw them, Arthur was only a matter of weeks old and we had the disastrous trip to the food festival. They tell me they were surprised I had wanted to go out and about when Arthur was so young. See, I was a doofus feeling like I had to be the hostess with the mostest when Arthur was so little. Their expectations were so different from what I thought I should be doing.

They thought I did really well that day and are surprised when I tell them everything that was going on in my head. It turns out mental ill health is so much easier to hide than something physical. And that really worries me. I was pretty open, talking to everyone I knew or didn't even know about how bad I felt after I had realised it wasn't baby blues. It makes me think about all the ladies who are suffering but not in here. I don't know who the 'brave' ones are or who the 'strong' ones are. If you can get through feeling so rubbish you want your life to end, day after day with no intervention, you must be flipping strong. It's just such a shame when there is no need. That's the way I see it and now I'm on the up trajectory, I'm determined to work in this field in the future. If talking about my experience can help just one person, make one person go to the doctor or take the bed that's being offered to them, then it will have been worth all of this.

We head to the towpath for a little walk before their long drive back to London. Coincidently, this is where Chris has been running in the morning as he's been working in Birmingham recently and staying in a hotel close by. What a small world it is, right? Imagine if I'd seen him or he'd seen me one of those mornings, we would have thought we were losing it, HA! We talk about the blind runner who runs every morning with a stick, who we have both obviously been impressed by.

We head back to the car park and I wave them off. It's been really good to see them but I'm not sad to wave them off. Yes, they are going back into the real world and I'm not, but I know it's a matter of days. I also know that they will end up in Cheltenham very soon. I know they want to start a family and I know they want to be close to Holly's family, so I just know I'll be seeing them so much more in the future.

15TH OCTOBER

Big ward round day. I'm so pleased to see Kim. I don't really know if it's allowed but the instant she steps into my room, I throw my arms round her. I feel like I'm her student and at this ward round meeting, I want to make her proud. We chat a bit and then she says she has to disappear off to talk to the other medical professionals about me. Apparently, the invite included my health visitor so she might be in the meeting room too.

About thirty minutes later, I'm called through. Walking up the corridor to the meeting room, I suddenly think back to the very first time I did this, shaking, feeling like everything was going in slow motion in the computer game I had found myself in and not knowing what was going to happen. This time, I have clothes on that make me feel like me, I have a bit of mascara on and I have dried my hair into an actual style. Furthermore, I know who is going to be in there and I know exactly what I'm going to say.

As I walk in, I see a sea of faces smiling at me (no health visitor). I beam back at them. We discuss the therapies that I had last week and that I'm still keen to go home tomorrow. They all look at each other, silently, but I know they are still in agreement too. Dr B says we'll stick with the plan that Rhys can pick us up tomorrow. We should take all our things from Room 7 but there will be a bed and a cot available for us for two weeks in case I feel like I want us to come back.

Everything inside me tingles and I'm pretty sure I'm about to cry. Looking at Kim tips me over the edge and I feel a big fat, wet tear fall out of my eye. It's a happy tear so without wiping it away, I spring up, say thank you and skip back to my room to tell Art the good news. We're finally going home for good. We'll see Daddy and Alma tomorrow and for every day after that.

Baby, we did it!

CHAPTER 9

LET MATERNITY LEAVE BEGIN

16TH OCTOBER

Right, gosh, well, I'd better get packing. Part of me can't believe I'm moving out, part of me thinks I've overstayed my welcome.

Rhys will be here in about two hours, so I'd best get this stuff sorted. I pull my dusty case out from under the bed.

The easy thing about packing to go home is that everything is going in, there is no choosing to do. I pop Arthur in his bouncy chair and turn BBC *Breakfast* on. He's mesmerised by the moving shapes and I'm once again relieved we haven't yet got to the point where we have to suffer *Peppa Pig*. He's still only four and a half months old.

Laura in organised mode is Laura at her best. I systematically go around emptying drawers and shelves. I left quite a few of my clothes at home last time so there really isn't that much to pack. Once all the clothes and toiletries are in the case, I move to the stuff on my windowsill. There is the canvas Rhys gave me for my birthday, a little trinket box one of the girls has made me and then there is a pile of papers. I sit down to go through them. Some are sheets we were given at the end of baby-massage classes. I keep them. I then get to a number of copies of my care plan and a number of copies of my rights with scribbled notes on that I made just before I went into ward-round meetings. I bin them.

Next are my psychology notes. I have pages and pages of CBT tables which I dive straight into reading. I have known about CBT for ages and find it really useful to stop in a situation and pick it apart as CBT would have us do. It just takes quite a bit of remembering to actually do that, rather than letting my brain just run away with the unhelpful thought, but I need to. I need to stop and check in with myself. Why am I feeling like this? What was the trigger? What are the unhelpful thoughts? What is the truth? Does the unhelpful thought still stand? It's a great technique that gets you thinking about the actual truth, not just what your head is telling you.

The notes make me realise what a long way I have come with not only confidence in myself but confidence with Arthur. There is no need to go over them in the future, they go in the bin.

As I'm pottering, Rhys appears at my door. I'm so pleased to see him and bound towards him for an excited hug. He's surprised I'm all packed up and I have no idea why – surely he wouldn't have expected anything less? As we are sat on the bed chatting, him recovering from the stress of the M5, a ghost-like figure appears at the door, pale and confused.

'Hello', I say.

Nothing.

Rhys and I look at each other and then both continue to smile at the figure. It feels like she might have been staring for about a minute, so we get up and continue to talk through what needs to go to the car. She stares for this whole time and then drifts off as silently as she had drifted in.

I realise that this ghost of a girl is just beginning on this hamster wheel. I'm about to be churned out the other end, having trusted the process and got to the point of being discharged to slip back into my life. I guess it just keeps going. Women keep having babies, brains keep malfunctioning and as long as the figure stays at one-in-five women, there are going to be new admissions and there are going to continue to be discharges. I wonder how long she'll be here. I wonder where she's come from. Poor thing. All of my heart feels for her.

As I take my things down to reception, Rhys packs the car up. When we are nearly done, I realise that I have forgotten about the things in the fridge and in the milk room. I make a bottle for Arthur in case we need it on the way home, knowing full well we won't as he is my robot baby. Now a fully functional mum, however, I will be prepared for any situation – you know, just in case.

In the kitchen, I find I have a box of peppermint tea and a jar of Marmite. There are going to be others who will be missing Marmite and will just want a peppermint tea one morning, so I leave both of them behind.

Taking a last walk down the corridor to Room 7, I have a little silent word with it from the doorway. 'Thanks, Room 7. I'm sure I'll miss you. By this time tomorrow, I'm sure you'll have someone new in here and I really hope they get better like me. Please make sure that happens to them, Room 7, please look after them.' At this point, Rhys and Arthur find me talking to an empty room and it really is time to go.

I'm not sure how I feel on the way home. I feel like I have left part of myself at The Barberry and if I think about that for too long, I get really sad about who I have left and the new, silent girl. I then force myself to think of the future. I think of the things I'll be able to do with Arthur now that I didn't do last time I was at home. I think of all the people I have missed and want to see. I think of being in our home and not being petrified. I'm looking forward to getting home and not feeling petrified. That's a good thing to look forward to, so I focus on that.

When we pull up onto the new drive, I smile. We're home. Rhys opens the door and Alma bundles out to see us both. He then goes around to the other side of the car to get Arthur out of the car seat. As he walks into our house with Arthur in his arms and Alma trotting next to him, I wish with all my might that this was about five months ago when we were coming home from the hospital. I'm calm and I'm collected. I just need to remember to take everything slowly.

But hey, it's not five months ago and, actually, if I really think about it, that's okay.

I follow them in with a new head, some new skills and pretty much a new way of looking at the world.

17TH OCTOBER

We had a calm first night back, but I did have a slight ding dong with Rhys. I've been arranging to see people and do things, but he thinks I should be taking it easy. I know he's right, but Normal Laura is one hundred miles an hour so taking it easy for me might appear to be doing too much for him. I know he's saying this because he cares and doesn't want me to undo all the good we have achieved. I assure him that I won't, and I'll make sure I sleep at some point when Arthur is sleeping too. End of discussion. He needs to look out for me, but he needs to trust that I will listen to my body and my mind and I will be more selfish in what I choose to go to and not go to.

19TH OCTOBER

Yesterday was a fine, staying-close-to-home pottering type of day. Today I've been out and the first weird thing happened. I know people generally mean well but today has been the first time I felt upset about being labelled as crazy. I'm not sure why as I'm keeping no secret of the fact that I have been away in hospital, but this really got to me.

I went to a yoga class. It was a mum class you could take babies to and I'd been emailing the instructor so she knew there was a possibility that if I felt like it was all just a bit too much, I might leave. And she was fine with that. It turns out that it was a very non-intimidating class. The instructor was just normal. She had normal gym gear on and her abs were safely tucked away. When I looked around, it seemed like everyone was pleased to be doing things with their baby, stopping to feed, comfort or give them toys whenever they had to. I was totally happy with this, I felt totally content and I decided I would make this a regular thing.

At the end of the class, I was popping Arthur in his pram to walk home and one of the other girls came over to me.

'I don't know if you remember me, we met in the park months ago.'

'Er, hmmm.'

'I'm in the same antenatal group as a friend of yours…'

'Oh yes, hello.' Oh gosh, this was the girl who had postnatal depression. My friend was going for coffee with her in the park months ago and, knowing I didn't feel great, she invited me. It was a totally lovely thing to do and I was really hoping to meet someone I would connect with, someone who got me, knew what I was feeling and we could make each other feel less alone.

She was nothing that I had hoped for. I'm not even sure if I said goodbye to her that day and if she hadn't come over, I would not have recognised her.

'I just wanted to say that, you know, I'm the one who is also a bit drrr, so there's no need to feel alone.' While saying this, she did the universal sign for 'crazy' you used to do when playing with other children in the playground when you were still young and innocent and knew no better – index finger making circle movements by the side of your head while your tongue pushes into the side of your bottom lip. I was dumbfounded. I had just had a really lovely yoga session with Arthur, in a new place which I'd got to all by myself. Now I felt tiny, and I felt incredibly angry. I'm not sure why entirely, but I knew it was something to do with the action she had just made. I took a deep breath and said thank you. I think the anger then took over as I let her know I'd just been discharged from an MBU where I'd been surrounded by many people who know exactly how I felt over the ten weeks I'd been there. I then hurriedly continued to pack the pram and make a quick exit. As I walked home, I felt tears bubbling up in my throat, but I was determined not to cry. She meant it in a nice way, she was trying to do a nice thing. And in all essence, it was, it just really got my goat.

As I walked home, I told myself not to give it a second thought and if she was there again, I would smile politely and just do me.

25TH OCTOBER

I have arranged to meet my antenatal class for coffee this morning. They are the first people I want to see. My baby crew. I want to see all of them and all of the babies and find out how we do this maternity-leave thing. Only a few of them are free but that's cool, I can't expect to click my fingers and for them to jump, not all of their lives have been on hold.

We agree to meet in a new café and I'm pleased about this. I like finding new places and it will be so good to go somewhere that doesn't have any memories associated with it. I'm not ready to try the car yet, so I pack everything I'll need, as opposed to leaving it to hope, and set off with Arthur.

As we walk down the street together, I look at Arthur in his pram and tell him I can't believe we're doing it, finally. I'm smiling, I look nice, I smell nice, I'm pleased to be with him. I think I'm mostly pleased that there will be decent coffee and a massive piece of cake at the end of this.

When I get there, the entrance is tiny and so is the café. I'm chilled about this, but I do wonder how we are going to get four prams in here. A waitress who I feel can sense my confusion tells me that there are meeting rooms behind the kitchen. Phew! We navigate around the coffee machine, which smells so good, and the whole place opens up to a big hall. It's called the School House Café, I should have guessed. I find two of the girls in a little room off the hall with sofas and loads of children's toys in. 'Well, isn't this nice?' I say. This to me means a lot of things. It's more than nice to see them, to be in a totally appropriate place with coffee and cake, to be *doing* maternity, to be out and about, to be not scared, to not feel like I'm a failure, to not think I'm a fraud, to be genuinely in the moment, seeing them, listening to them. I hug them both as a third joins us. We get our things from the café and I mostly listen to them all just having normal chat about how they are getting on and what's going on for them with their little ones at the moment. They have asked how I am, but I'm pleased it's not been an interview. I'm totally happy to tell them anything about what it's been like in Birmingham but I'm so pleased to just listen to the normal mum chat, you wouldn't believe. They have been doing this for months now, this is just their new normal so I'm conscious that I need to contain my enthusiasm, be chilled and just go with it.

I put Arthur in his pram for a nap and realise I'm feeling tired too. So, with Rhys in my head, I tell them I'm going to make a move. They all agree that they probably should be going too, so we leave together, hug and walk off in our separate directions. The fresh air wakes me up so, as I walk home, I potter in a few of the shops on the way, just pleased to be doing me.

26TH OCTOBER

Today is the day. Today is the day I do Buggyfit. I have always loved running and generally keeping fit. I don't know if it's the 'it' that I like doing or the feeling afterwards. Regardless, I need it back in my life and one of the goals from my care plan is to get to a class.

Kim has texted to ask if I want her to come round this morning. I thought about it but told her I really wanted to do this class and a new friend, Amy, who I had met just before having Arthur, had arranged to go with me. She totally understood and told me she would see me next week. Good, right decision, Laura, confirmed.

I've arranged to meet Amy by the church between our two roads. The plan is to walk the forty minutes to the class, get a feed in before it starts and then the babies would hopefully sleep or at least be content for the whole class. Amy would normally drive but I'm still not keen on using the car, so we are walking. I feel bad about this, but she seems enthusiastic to give it a go. If this doesn't help me burn the extra stone that is hospital biscuits and cake, I don't know what will.

When we get there, I'm again so relieved I'm bottle-feeding. I totally admire Amy for still breastfeeding, and in sports stuff, but I'm totally content to use a bottle. Most importantly, I don't feel like a failure.

I fill in a form that asks about the amount of sleep I'm getting, what kind of delivery I had, if I'm breastfeeding and if I'm on any medication. I'm good on the sleep (thankfully), I had a horrific delivery but my caesarean section is now nearly five months old, I'm not breastfeeding but I'll need about ten minutes to fill in the medication section. When I hand the form in, the instructor asks about the effects of the medication and obviously, I tell the whole story. I am happy to. I guess if I tell the leader of a mum's group what

I've been through, maybe she'll be able to help me 'get to' mums who might be struggling too.

I can't tell you how much I enjoyed the class. It was such a variety of all things, bodyweight strength exercises, running, walking between stations, stretching. I don't really know what I expected but I was surprised how much distance we covered, and I was very surprised when one of the circuits involved a run around the lake. I would have thought the last bit of running I'd done on my own down the canal would have prepared me for this but there is nothing like a herd of mums powering around a lake. A chance to have a bit of a competition and do something for yourself, they were awesome. I brought up the rear and felt like I was about to pass out when I got back to the pack but that was okay – I made it around and I am not a failure. We finished with some stretches and the teacher checked my tummy for separation before it was then time for Amy and I to walk the forty minutes home uphill – I'm not surprised Amy normally drives.

Thankfully, there was a little coffee shop in the park, so we treated ourselves to skinny cappuccinos and off we wandered through town, up home. I felt accomplished, I felt like I had given everything, and I felt like we had cemented a friendship, or at least I know we are now in a coffee round – that's friendship, right?

Amy and I first started talking as we both had small babies. She'd lent me some tiny clothes and told me that tiny baby nappies existed. She was like my coach in what to do with a little baby and she sympathised that they ate ALL of the time when they were little. Every midwife I had seen in hospital who saw his birth weight had commented, 'He'll be a hungry baby' and they were not wrong. Amy's son arrived six weeks early, so she had experienced a number of weeks in an intensive-care unit. We had both been through tough baby-related times early on and I guess this will always bond us.

By the time I got home and showered it was nearly 13:00, I couldn't believe it. I'm not surprised the days just go when you're on maternity leave. I had booked myself a hair appointment for this afternoon and Rhys was going to come home early from work so he could be with Arthur and I could really enjoy the pampering. I felt totally drained from the morning's exertions. At least all I had to do this afternoon was sit and talk about things that neither of us really wanted to talk about. No, I won't do that. The new selfish me will ask for a magazine with pictures in it which I'll enjoy looking at. I will keep what I'm doing this evening and where we are planning to go on holiday to myself.

I did just that, told the hairdresser to do what they wanted while I quaffed more coffee, which turned into Prosecco once I told them why I wanted a total change (all right, I can't not chat for that long…) and pretty much stumbled out of there!

Rhys met me halfway home with Arthur and Alma and we had a delightfully cosy night in with my newly chopped, newly blonded, newly me hair.

27TH OCTOBER

Richard and Lou are back from their Europe trip and are staying with us for a few nights. I'm so pleased I get the opportunity to see them, as what I would consider to be Normal Laura again. I can cook for them; I can plan trips for us all and I'm back in my element. Tomorrow is the Suffolks' Street Fair. It's on about four times a year and it's pretty much always the same stalls but there are lots of food stalls and there is usually live music and I would consider it good and British, so they will love that.

28TH OCTOBER

I was looking forward to the street fair but excitement went through the roof when I got there and saw there was a dog competition running for charity – brilliant! I entered Alma into the Prettiest Bitch and Waggiest Tail classes. She's had her tail docked but what she's got she can wag. There was no Paralympic event so she's going in with the big guns.

As we wander through the fair, Richard and I have a mulled wine and Alma gets offered a homemade vegan dog treat, which she promptly spits out. *Oh, Alma, you eat fox poo, surely you can handle this, you're so embarrassing.* I feel like I am apologising to a friend's mum about something they have cooked that Arthur doesn't like. We thank them, talk about how fussy our dog is and quickly move on.

Just before show time, Rhys manages to join us from work and takes Alma forward to the ring once they announce the Prettiest Bitch category. I size up the competition – mainly little things: pugs, French bulldogs, sausages. I think we've got this. Nope, the sausage wins. Don't worry, Alma, it's completely down to this guy from the vet's surgery and he just pandered to the crowd.

Waggiest Tail next, we have to win it. Rhys manages to source a tennis ball. We are in with a chance, Alma lives for tennis balls. When they call her name out, he produces the ball and her little nubby tail goes wild. She is a total crowd-pleaser; everyone loves an underdog.

SHE WINS! We are all over the moon, so proud of our Alma. As the vet steps forward to congratulate her, I see he has a box – well done, Alma! He pins a rosette on her collar and gives the box to Rhys and tells him not to let her have them all at once. As I go to hug them both, I look at Alma's prize – a whole box of vegan treats. *Oh, Alma!*

29TH OCTOBER

Big day today. Granddad and Lou are looking after Arthur while Rhys and I truck back to Birmingham. I'm not packing an overnight bag. I can't see any reason they won't discharge me. We both look smart as we have been told to be as late as we want to be getting back tonight. Without talking about it, I reckon we have both dressed up, for each other and for ourselves. After the appointment in Birmingham, we've planned to drive home to Cheltenham, leave the car at home and walk to a restaurant – just the two of us – for dinner and drinks. We've not done this for months. Well, probably closer to a year if you count pregnancy as I wasn't a fun date through the whole of that either, what with the morning sickness that quickly turned into heartburn.

We're at the hospital and I'm not quite sure how to introduce myself to the main receptionist. 'We're here for a meeting with Dr Berrisford in The Chamomile Suite, please.'

'No problem, I'll just let his secretary know you are here, please take a seat.'

So we do.

I'm relieved we're waiting in the main reception. I'm not sure if I am ready to see Room 7 with a new inhabitant in, or see any of my fellow inmates and for them to feel sad that I am out and they are still in. A familiar nurse comes to pick us up and take us through to the oh-so-familiar ward-round meeting room, where I clap eyes on Kim and Dr B straight away. Everyone is smiling.

'You look great! How's it been going at home?' Dr B starts the meeting.

'I feel great, thank you. I've done all sorts, met up with friends, been to yoga and Buggyfit. And Rhys's dad and his partner are back staying with us, so we've been to a street fair with them and plan to go to Westonbirt Arboretum with them tomorrow.'

'Okay,' he says, looking at Rhys. 'That doesn't sound like a slow ramp up back into your usual life…'

To which Rhys promptly comes back in his usual jokey way with, 'I told you! I knew you were doing too much.'

Everyone laughs as I protest, and we have a debate around my version of taking it slow and everyone else's version of the same statement.

Dr B calls a halt on the debate and, with a smile on his face, says, 'You do have to remember how ill you have been, Laura. You've been in a Mother and Baby Unit for nearly three months. We keep these beds for the most poorly mums, so please don't underestimate that.'

'I know,' I say, looking at my hands. 'I appreciate that I don't want to undo all the good work we have done, and I promise I'll only organise one thing a day. I think I've just been excited to be back and I'm conscious that I don't have that much maternity leave left. But I do still feel tired so I am still trying to be home over lunchtime so I can nap when Arthur does.'

'Okay.' He's quiet for a while. 'How have work been? If you need me to write a letter to support your case for having longer than a year off, I'm more than happy to. You have spent a lot of your maternity leave in hospital and I think it's really important that you have some time just with Arthur and as a family before you go back to work. This is an important time in your recovery.'

'Thank you, I'd like that. I'm sure they will be fine as I have kept my boss up to date all the way through and he's been really supportive. But yes, please, it would be good to have your letter of support.'

Dr B makes a note and then looks back up. 'Now, last thing on my list, and I have to say this. Please, what's happened here, this should not put you off considering having another child.'

I immediately laugh and make it clear there is not a chance, I'm NEVER having another child.

Then I look at Rhys and he's not laughing. I feel a bit silly, stop talking and look back at Dr B.

'I know no one wants to hear that, just as they are being discharged from here, but I have to say it as, if you were to fall pregnant, you would be on Kim and her team's radar.' He looks at Kim and she nods in agreement. 'What's happened to you was totally out of the blue. And if it did happen again, we'd be prepared for it. You obviously don't need to and probably don't want to be thinking about other children right now. You may or may not feel differently the more time you spend away from here, but I need to tell you that.'

'Okay, thank you.' I nod, more soberly this time.

And with that, Dr B looks around the room and asks if there is anything else anyone wants to raise. There isn't. He asks if we have any questions. I look at Rhys and he simply says, 'Go on then, give him a hug!'

We all laugh and I obviously burst into tears. As the tears run down my cheeks, I throw my arms around Dr B. I cannot thank this man enough. He's made the right calls at the right time. He's been human, he's been kind and I have hung on his every word. It's truly amazing when you meet people like this. People you trust to the end and will do anything they suggest, despite only knowing them a number of minutes.

I sit back down and Rhys picks up my hand to continue holding it in his. We say our goodbyes and thank yous again and I ask the nurse to take the tins of chocolates and gossip magazines I've brought onto the ward as a small gesture of my thanks. I mean, how do you thank a team of people who have contributed towards saving your life? I know chocolates and new magazines to replace the ones talking about Katie Price's second wedding isn't much, but I hope they will bring smiles to their faces.

As the same nurse who brought us down escorts us back to the main reception, we thank her again for everything, and I of course give her a hug before walking through the sliding doors. As we step outside, I see the deaf chap, dancing away but solo this time. I flash him a smile, wave goodbye and I know he doesn't have a clue who I am.

In the car on the way home, I sleep.

My body is physically and emotionally drained. Every muscle is still stiff from the assault that was Buggyfit. I don't think I have done that many lunges or squats in an hour in my life. But more importantly, after that appointment at The Barberry, I feel that – happy or sad –there are no more tears to cry.

***

I know we are heading into a whole new chapter of our lives. It's coming three months after we thought it would be, but it's coming and I'm excited for it.

Tonight in Cheltenham, we are having Thai. Having had hospital food for the best part of three months, I'm desperate to have something that's not mashed potato or custard. Don't get me wrong, I live for pudding, but me and custard are going to have to take a short break. Rhys and I manage one espresso martini after dinner and then, after all the emotional turmoil, we both know it's definitely time to call it a night. As we walk through the front door at home, Richard and Lou are really surprised. It's 20:00. They didn't expect us back until after they had gone to bed.

As Rhys tells them all about the meeting, I slip off upstairs to see our little bug. I've missed him. I think this day trip might have been the longest I have spent away from him. He's sleeping soundly, lips pursed, his little arms above his head and I just stare at him and promise him things are going to be better from now on.

I can't drag my eyes off him. He looks so content and I feel so content knowing we are back where we belong, in our home as a family. I get the rush of love. I totally get it. It didn't come on day one for me but at this moment, staring at him, I love him so much it actually hurts.

As I wash my face and brush my teeth, I reflect on our date night. (I feel like me reflecting on things is going to be a big part of my life now.) We did have a nice night. I hate that adjective but that's the only word I can come up with to describe it. The food was tasty, the wine went down very well and I wouldn't have wanted to be there with anyone else. But I guess there are a lot of unspoken words between Rhys and me. We've got through it, for sure, we have done that. We've done all the things that have been asked of us and we have definitely got to the other end of this bit and we're living together in the same beautiful house with our adorable baby son and a dog with the waggiest tail in Cheltenham. But there are these unspoken words.

What happened all that time I was in hospital? How is Rhys actually doing? Does he ever think about the things I said I wanted to do to myself and to Arthur? Will he ever forget that, and will he ever be able to look at me the same way? Does he still want to marry me?

How do I feel about him? I've lived without him for so long. Do I blame him in any way? Should we have let his mum and Bernard leave when they were going to? Should I have been left to handle things on my own without 'babysitters'? Would that have helped me, or would that have made it worse?

These were subjects to be avoided on our first date in a million years and I guess our conversation was superficial because we both understood this. This stuff will come up at some point and we do need to talk about it. We can't march on and forget about it, well, I know I can't. And I know we will never know the answers to some of these things swirling around in my head and that's just going to have to be fine.

If there is one thing I have learned, I must not worry about the things out of my control. There is zero point, none.

This will have to be the first of many dates. We can do stupid chat for the first few for sure, as that's what you do. Then, in order to move on and to let this chapter go, I know we will have to start to understand how living through this has been for each other. I know it will be painful and insightful in equal measure, but there is only one thing for it. We will have to make time for ourselves and we will have to get to know each other all over again.

EPILOGUE

When I hear Arthur cry now, I feel an actual physical pain in my chest. Every part of my being wants to make the tears stop. When he's ill, I want it to be me. When he falls over, I want to be able to kiss it better. Pick-up from nursery is now truly the most magical part of the day. His smile when he sees me is worth all the money in this world. The hug and the sloppy open-mouthed kisses I will take over and over again. They are like a tonic, something that makes me feel whole and complete.

I'm just desperately sorry that I don't get the opportunity to go back. To feel what it's like to have that kind of love at the beginning. To feel that connection. To not be petrified of everything and not to dream of cutting my own wrists. But that time has gone now. I don't blame anyone that it happened, I don't blame anyone at all. I didn't have the most conventional of maternity leaves, but in a very odd way, I feel like I'm in a special club of people. I'm in a club where I know what it's like to feel so desperate and I now have tools to help me cope with that. And with this knowledge comes immense power. I now have the power to help other women. I am the hope that they maybe need to see, to trust they will get better.

And if I had to do it all over again to gain this power, I would. I would do it over and over and over again. Yes, I am sorry that I didn't have that time, but I have the power to help other families get that time back and that feels pretty special.

I know you're all wondering about a few things, so let me help you out, starting of course with the most important:

Alma Poor Alma, she's been through it all with us. She ended up having a second operation to sort her scarring problem out. She still has the waggiest nub in Cheltenham, having regained the title at The Exmouth Pub in 2019. She's my constant and I think I do actually love that dog as much as I could love a human. On days when I've had it bad, she has been by my side. On days when I've felt like I couldn't leave the house but really do have to, she's come with me. Seeing her and Arthur grow up together is the most heart-warming thing you will ever see. Alma is constantly fed up of him hitting her or trying to ride her, but she takes it all in her stride and continues to wag.

Arthur He is now two years old and, to me, he is the most adorable thing on this planet. He is of course a terror and there are times when I just need to walk away from him – being a parent is hard! But the good times outweigh the bad and if there is something that's particularly bad going on – like the biting stage we are in now – I keep telling myself it will end. He won't walk into secondary school and bite his teachers when they ask him to do something he doesn't want to do (or at least I hope not!). Everyone who tells you 'It's a phase', I know it is annoying at the time but they are right, it really is. He's at nursery full time and he loves it. He has actual pals who he babbles about and thank goodness their parents are pretty cool so it's okay to hang out on weekends too ;-).

Rhys is good. He's still taking the Sertraline and it's not a secret, he's just not as open about any of this stuff, unless there is a particular need to be. This was such a painful time for him, he doesn't see any need in reliving it. And that's fine for now. Because of the pain I saw in him and continue to see, I will continue to push the agenda of *help for partners*. I always hated that all the focus was on me but understand why it needed to be, I was the priority. But he has suffered and continues to suffer. He continues to question if I'm doing too much but that's just the way I operate. At least he's keeping an eye on me! We keep an eye on each other.

Me I'm good too, thanks! Work have been so understanding with me. I did get my three-month extension to maternity leave and went back on a very gradual, phased return. I'm now back to working five days a week and my confidence is back to where it was. I don't know if this is how every parent feels but I don't stress as much about work things any more. I just do what needs to be done to the best of my ability and then I come away. Gone are the days of working through the night or constantly checking my work emails over the weekend. No one from work will ever need me that badly or for something to be done that quickly. I don't believe it. I do really like what I do but it's not the priority any more and I won't break any of my relationships for it.

What's helped me really enjoy work is that I've been really open with what happened to me and, consequently, have found like-minded people. A colleague in the London office started a group called 'Great Minds' and I now run a programme of events for the Gloucester office, Great Minders, on his behalf. It's the group's aim to get rid of the stigma around talking about mental health, in particular talking about it at work. We have trained mental health first aiders in all offices globally, as well as the regular physical first aiders. We run a monthly programme of wellness and mental-health-related events which range from meditation and Pilates to hearing from a colleague about their lived experience with a hidden illness or caring for a loved one. This is the most rewarding thing I have ever done in my working life and I think it makes me enjoy the 'bread and butter' project stuff more.

Running I continue to run. In fact, I was so keen to get back to half-marathon distance that I entered the Cheltenham half marathon again, which was in September the following year. The keenness meant I went too far too quickly and managed to develop a stress fracture about two months before the race. Needless to say, I ended up wearing an orthopaedic boot on my wedding day. But, not to worry, Bec managed to trip over some tree roots the week before the wedding on a run of her own, so her face scab distracted from my fractured foot – what a pair! With the consultant's blessing, I wore my dream wedding shoes down the aisle and then swapped them over for the dancing. I wouldn't change a thing!

Marriage So, yes. Rhys and I did get married and it was the best TWO days of our lives (so far). We couldn't get all those Australians over from Melbourne and not throw a long, extended event for them, showing the best of British hospitality, could we?! The day we did the legal stuff, Alma was on the front row with Arthur and Mum and George. I walked down the aisle to 'Girl on Fire' by Alicia Keys in a See By Chloé dress and dreamy Valentino shoes (thanks, Dad) and despite not losing all that hospital weight, I felt a million dollars. And of course, there was not a dry eye in the house. I'm not sure if it was Bec or me who started everyone else off.

It took me about three minutes of looking at my dad and digging my fingers into his arm before I could take a step down the aisle. I think the raw emotion of everything we had been through hit me in that second, hearing that song. We went for tapas in a local restaurant with the wedding party for our wedding breakfast. After the meal, Rhys and I with my mum and George walked home merry as can be with 12 helium balloons between us spelling out MR & MRS HOPPER.

The next day, we threw a party in an old brewery. I drove myself, my bridesmaids (Bec and Ellie of course) and Alma to the venue, where I knew Rhys was going to be performing his 'secret hobby'. As the three of us walked in, hand in hand, and Alma wrestled with her eucalyptus collar outside, the crowds parted and Rhys was sat at a piano playing AND singing Elton John's 'Your Song'. Again, not a dry eye in the house. The chat was excellent, the speeches even better, we toasted with espresso martinis and the band tried to keep up with Lyds and her rendition of 'Proud Mary' into the small hours. I will remember those two days for ever.

Our Relationship And on the more serious stuff, we are yet to find a relationship counsellor in Cheltenham we gel with, so we'll continue to try to work stuff out together until we do. Communication is key, it's just a shame we forget about that every now and again.

Australia In March 2019, I'm so pleased to say that we did indeed make the 27-hour trip to Melbourne. And there, Arthur met his namesake, Great-Granddad Arthur. They high-fived and it was a magical moment. To this day, GG Arthur still talks about Arthur as 'a firecracker'.

Drugs Back home, and about a year after being discharged from hospital, I managed to come off the night-time drug

Mirtazapine successfully. I say successfully but I did have a minor wobble over Christmas 2019, but I think it was just the whole Christmas and New Year thing. I went back to see my original doctor and she decided I needed some time out and we wouldn't make a knee-jerk reaction and go back on to Mirtazapine. She kept an eye on me and, after a week, she signed a fit note for me to again make a gradual return to working life. Since then, I have had my 18-month check with Dr Morgan in Cheltenham, and we have decided that I'll stay on the same (maximum) dose of Venlafaxine I left the hospital on for another six months. I do have good and bad days, but I am so lucky that I have a great, open relationship with work and if I need to take a sick day I will. I don't take the piss, but I also know that sitting at my desk not being able to concentrate or having a panic attack in the loo isn't going to help anyone.

And so, here we are now. Our family, the four of us. Writing this book has helped no end in thinking that one day there could be five of us. But time, as they say, will tell…

It is okay to be a mum and ask for help.

It is okay to be a mum and admit you don't really like having a baby, and it's even okay to be a mum and admit that you don't want to be on this planet any more. This is not a weakness, something to be ashamed of and to hide from the world. You owe it to yourself; you owe it to your partner; you owe it to your little family to tell someone. You don't have to tell the world, but please, just tell someone. Tell someone, get the help you need. Then, I promise, you will be able to enjoy being a mother and feel like all of those adverts you see. Not every day. Of course not every day. But the good will outweigh the bad and the love you feel for that little one will be like something you have never experienced.

If it's the shame associated with admitting it happened to you, well, then, let's do something about that. I know it won't change overnight but please, let's all try to make it okay to talk about this stuff. Not just mental health in general, as trendy as it is right now, but specifically perinatal mental health. You can be old, you can be young, you can be on your first or fifth child. You can be an admin assistant, a doctor, a supermarket worker, a plumber, a vet or still looking for the right job. This illness does not discriminate. Women don't 'get this' because of who they are, what they have done or not done, it's just an illness that needs treating like any other.

Let's get that out there and let it be known.

Dear Arthur,

The whole time I have been writing, you have of course been front and centre of my mind. I know you will read this when you are old enough and that scares me to death. But there was no point in going through this and no good coming of it.

I'm sorry. I'm sorry that this happened to me and that I had those thoughts about you. I know sorry doesn't even cover it. I hope that every day you know how much you mean to me. I wish I had felt the love I feel for you now from the minute you were born. But I didn't, and there is no point in wishing that as nothing will change it. All of my energy is now focused on you and trying to turn what was a truly horrid six months of our lives into a positive.

I hope you are proud of me. Proud of me for getting help and getting better, and proud of me for sharing our story in the hope of helping other women and other families. I know you will be proud of Daddy for how he coped. He loves you more than anything in this world and he did from the moment you entered it.

I promise I'll do my best to teach you that it's okay to ask for help if you need it. I know you'll be kind and caring and I couldn't ask for any more. I also know you'll be a well-rounded boy. What with a mummy who talks a lot about mental health and a daddy who thinks you should try everything at least once, how could you not be?

I'm proud of what we have achieved together.

I love you, baby boy.

Mummy x

RESOURCES

UK

NHS 111
Call 111 if you have an urgent medical problem and you're not sure what to do.

NHS 999
Call 999 in a medical emergency.

Your local GP
You have the legal right to choose a GP practice that best suits your needs. www.nhs.uk/service-search/find-a-gp

PANDAS
PND Awareness and Support. pandasfoundation.org.uk / 0808 1961 776

NHS urgent mental health helpline
For help during a mental-health crisis or emergency, 24-hour advice, 7 days a week. www.nhs.uk/service-search/mental-health/find-an-urgent-mental-health-helpline/

Qwell

Online counselling, peer support and self-help resources; no referral needed.
www.qwell.io/

Baby Buddy app

Free NHS-accredited, multi-award-winning, interactive pregnancy and parenting app with 24-hour text messaging support.
Available from www.nhs.uk/apps-library/, the App Store (Apple), or Google Play (Android)

DadPad app

The essential guide for new dads, developed with the NHS.
Available from the App Store (Apple), or Google Play (Android)

Home Start

Parenting support charity.
www.home-start.org.uk/

Family Action

Family information service providing practical, emotional and financial support to those who are experiencing poverty, disadvantage and social isolation across the country.
www.family-action.org.uk/

Bluebell

Charity supporting families dealing with depression and anxiety related to pregnancy and birth.
bluebellcare.org/

AUSTRALIA

PANDA

Perinatal Anxiety & Depression Australia. Includes a national perinatal mental health helpline.
www.panda.org.au/
1 300 726 306 /
support@panda.org.au

Centre of Perinatal Excellence

Charity providing support for the emotional challenges of becoming a parent. Includes a 'Getting help' page.
www.cope.org.au/

Gidget Foundation Australia

A not–for–profit organisation providing programmes to support the emotional wellbeing of expectant and new parents.
gidgetfoundation.org.au/

Beyond Blue

Australian mental-health charity providing a Support Service via a 24/7 telephone helpline, daily web chat (between 3pm–12am) and email (with a response provided within 24 hours).
www.beyondblue.org.au/
get–support / 1 300 22 4636

ACKNOWLEDGEMENTS

It's not much of an exaggeration to say that the first version of these acknowledgements was nearly as long as the book itself. It was then that I was gently reminded that this section is dedicated to thanking those who have supported me in creating this book. I really hope, therefore, that I have already thanked all those who supported me in the story you have just read – more than once, and in person. You can be confident that you were in the first version of these acknowledgements.

Now focus, Canty. The people I would like to thank for supporting me in creating this book are:

Rhys, my husband. We are probably on opposite ends of the 'share everything–keep everything private' spectrum so I don't underestimate how big a deal it is for you to put this out there. Thank you for supplying me with snacks and hugs as I tap, tap, tapped away in the little box room. Sorry for leaving you wifeless for many weekends. Thank you for being on the front line with me, for looking after the stranger who had suddenly appeared in your house, for coming to the appointments, for saying the right things and for being the most huggable you.

Thank you to Bec and Ellie, the main 'pal characters' in this book. I don't know what I did to deserve you. You know what I'm thinking (so can follow my winding stories), you know what to do to help and, more importantly, you were always there, working with us as a family. You will always be part of our family. Thank you for helping me piece the story together, for reading the same bits over and over and for always asking how it's going. This is our book for sure! Oh, and Bec, never stop crying at random things, please.

Rosie, book-club leader extraordinaire. Thank you for thinking of me this whole time and being the most excited person, from the moment I told you I was going to try to do this. Thank you for reading all the versions and all the proposals and I'm sorry most of it was rubbish in the early days! I love that our book club is just a bunch of pals who come together (semi) regularly to catch up on their actual lives and perhaps talk about a book we may or may not have read. May it never change. And please, girls, don't be too harsh on this one.

Sophie Bradshaw, my agent (I can hear myself saying that and I feel very big headed). I am so pleased I found you. When I sent the speculative enquiry on your website, I didn't think that a few days later we would be sat in a coffee shop in Stroud talking about our experiences of becoming mums. I still remember the moment you said you would like to represent me and driving home with the biggest grin on my face. You have the passion I have for perinatal mental health and what you don't know about writing books isn't worth knowing; that's how we got to this point. Thank you for all your hard work – I certainly, definitely could not have done it without you, FACT.

Jake and your team at Monoray, thank you, thank you, thank you for giving us this platform. Thank you for taking a punt on a nobody from the north who had a story she wanted to tell. Sophie and I knew it would just take one and that's what kept us going. We always had faith that someone would realise the importance of what we had to say. Thank you for being that one. You gave us the time of day and very much share our passion for trying to give hope to mums and families through this book.

Now I'm straying a little off topic, but I absolutely cannot miss a few more…

To all the amazing ladies and the few brave men who work on the Chamomile Suite. I know some crappy gossip magazines and a couple of tins of chocolate will never cut it, but I really don't know how to thank you. You are all very special and are making a massive difference to people's lives. I know you know that, but I hope I have done you justice in writing some of it down. And to Dr B – I wouldn't have stayed and got back to me if it wasn't for you. You and your team are priceless, thank you.

Thank you to my amazing GP, Dr Cox. You got it from the minute I walked in the door and I can never thank you enough for not making me feel like anything other than a woman who needed help. You handled our case with compassion and kindness and I always feel safe in your hands.

To the Crisis and Perinatal Team and to Kim in particular, you are wonderful. I know you would never want to be singled out for something you do as your job, but I am doing just that because you are just flipping brilliant. And to Trish, thanks for having me as a volunteer. I love every moment I work with you and your team.

Last and by no means least, thank you to my parents: my mum, my dad and my stepdad. Now I am a parent, I know how much I would have hurt and worried you. I now know what you mean when you say you would rather it be you.

Mum, my mum, the sweetest, most positive, enthusiastic person I know. I know I put you through hell, but not once did you let me see I was breaking you. Now that's strong. Thank you for raising a strong one; I know we will always support each other through whatever comes our way. And thank you to George for always selflessly supporting your wife, my mum, in putting me first, despite fighting your own battle and needing her support more than ever.

Dad, thank you for being so chilled through all this. Thank you for coming to see us and helping in any way you could – from stopping to pick up washing powder, to putting up blinds, to saying the right things at the right time. I can't imagine how surreal and upsetting it must have been seeing your only daughter go to pieces. All those miles on the motorway travelling to see us at home and in hospital got us there.

Gosh, that was heavy…Come on, Alma, time for some fresh air.